Ask Raphael

A Conversation with the Archangel
Channeled by Betty Rae, B.S., M.Ed.

Ask Raphael

Transcribed by Betty Rae

© Copyright 2020 by Betty Rae, B.S., M.Ed., C. T.

All rights reserved. No part of this book may be used or reproduced by any means, graphic, electronic, or mechanical including photocopying, recording, taping or by any information storage retrieval system without the written permission of the author except in the case of brief quotations embodied in articles and reviews.

ISBN: 9798727910665

Table of Contents

An Introduction by Betty Rae 1

An Introduction by Raphael 3

Chapter 1 Who am I? 9

Chapter 2 What is a Soul? 25

Chapter 3 Why Do People Do Terrible Things to
One Another? 33

Chapter 4 What About My Physical Body? 52

Chapter 5 What About My Brain? 63

Chapter 6 What is Spirit Consciousness? 77

Chapter 7 Why Did Pandora Open That Darn Box? 89

Chapter 8 Why Do I Have Dreams? 99

Chapter 9 What is My Purpose For Being Here? 111

Chapter 10 How Can I Be Happy When...? 117

Chapter 11 What About My Work And Career? 123

Chapter 12 What About Relationships? 129

Chapter 13 How Do I Win At Life's Games? 147

Chapter 14 How Do I Hear My Guardian Angel? 161

Chapter 15 How Do I Unlock The Power of My
Imagination? 165

Chapter 16 How Do I Create A Happy Home? 177

Chapter 17 What About Different Forms of Divination?.......185

Chapter 18 What About Prayer and Meditation? 201

Chapter 19 How Do I Interpret the Symbols? 215

Chapter 20 More Guided Mediations 229

Chapter 21 What Happens When I Die? 257

Chapter 22 How Do I Find Happiness?!..................................277

Chapter 23 A New Earth..299

Acknowledgements 303

About the Author...305

An Introduction by Betty Rae

This book is a recording of the wisdom channeled through me by the Archangel Raphael in answer to the many questions of the thousands of people who have come to us. The clear and loving messages always lifted their hearts and minds through this healing angel's guidance.

Rather than constantly saying who is speaking, I've decided to put my questions as well as those by our many clients into *italicized font* and Raphael's words in another font to make it easier to read and discern who is speaking.

Although there are many names people give for God such as "Allah," "Heavenly Father," "Buddha," "Isis," "Great Spirit," "Krishna," "Christ," "The Source," and still more with each religion to assemble in the name of a "Higher Power," Raphael has chosen to use the most recognized ones in English-speaking countries: "God," "Creator," and "Higher Power." I have asked that we use the capitalized non-gender pronoun "It" when we speak of God.

Because angels and archangels are pure spirit, they are also non-gender, but for this book, we will use the male pronoun for Raphael so as not to confuse the pronoun It for God.

Again, we will show our questions and comments in italics.

Raphael and I are here to assist you, dear reader. Call upon God, the Source of all that is, to reveal to you all you are now and will become. God will send Its Archangels for your enlightenment.

Although Raphael has likely been with me since birth, I was not aware of the archangel until about fifty years ago when I began hearing his voice within me. It frightened me at first until I settled down to accept the gentle words and great wisdom given through me for others. Then, in 1995, words flowed through me in the form of letters that were signed, "Your Guardian Angel." It is now available on my web page entitled, "Letter from a Guardian Angel."

Now in my 80's, there is an urgency to record the wisdom of this angelic being before I pass from this earth. Yet, I have questioned Raphael, "How on earth can you capsulize billions of years of our physical life experiences as humans?"

This giant being of divine light simply said, "With the first word."

As channeling becomes more widely accepted and as we write this in the year 2020, I know it is the right time to bring forth an archangel's wisdom. It is urgently needed to solve global warming that is threatening our very existence. As if that were not enough, at the time of this writing, the world is experiencing the Coronavirus that has stopped us in our tracks. In all my years, I have never seen such pandemic ravish human populations all over the world.

When I asked Raphael, "What in the world is going on?"

He said, "It is the time of times when your human population is raising its consciousness. It is a time when your Earth is cleansing itself of old ideas and bringing forth an insurgence of the new."

Raphael is always quick to point out the good that can come even from a pandemic. For example, the isolation turns one to prayer and meditation.

Through it all, Raphael sends forth these uplifting messages to inspire us, to heal our physical, mental, and emotional bodies, and to bless our humanity with inner peace and joy.

An Introduction by Raphael

We are Raphael, God's messenger of healing to the human race. We are a being of divine light who brings forth the mind of God into all languages for the advancement of humankind.

Rae is but one of our many channels translating God's thoughts and ideas.

We speak in the pronoun **we** to denote that all within the angelic realm are of one mind and purpose to serve God.

Indeed, in this book, we have set forth the task of redefining previously held beliefs. Humans tend to label everything. Long ago, your ancestors named those of us in the angelic realm as the Choir of Angels portraying us in various ranks before the throne of God. This is a lovely imagery, but we are far more than this. God designed Its angelic realm as translators of divine Mind to reach all of Its creations.

We do not wear wings. Again, the human image of authors describing battles between good and evil set forth this image as truth. It is not.

Although many venerate us, we insist that we are no greater or lesser than you or any of God's creations. We are God's messengers to your world to translate the God Mind into your human languages and to bring an awakening of your Oneness within the Creator of us all. We are speaking through this channel to raise your consciousness so you may experience divine harmony, peace, love, and joy within your dear self. While you cannot yet escape the experience of the turmoil and darkness of your Earth's polarities, sooner or later you are destined to enter into full awareness of the joy of divine light that is God. You call this *Enlightenment*. We call this *The Awakening*. Once reached, your explorations of your planet will conclude and you will ascend to the higher realms of sentient beings.

Be of good heart, dear souls. From the first lifetime as a sentient being you entered the physical world clad in a space-suit called your physical body. Long ago, beings from another planet came to prepare Earth to receive you. You remember these beings as gods described in both your Roman and Greek mythology.

You are scientists exploring a planet. With each visit, your experiences gain your soul knowledge in how to use God's energy to create within the confines of a planet that has both positive and negative polarities. It is not an easy path and this is most likely not your last lifetime. Although Earth may seem like a school for souls, it is more like a science laboratory where your choices become an experiment from which you gain new knowledge which leads to better experiments which lead to wisdom and eventually mastership. There is no "pass/fail" for advancement.

When you begin to see God in everyone and everything, when you cease to judge your life or the lives of others and come to love and enjoy each moment of your existence upon your beautiful planet, and when you can manifest all your needs, then you will know it is your last time of exploring your planet. And even when you accomplish this, like many advanced souls on your planet now, you may choose to return to help those souls still exploring the planet to speed the healing of your Earth.

We urge you to let go of fear and anxiety for yourself, for others and for your planet. Use your powerful ability to create beauty and goodness first within yourself and then allow your love to bring light to others all across your world.

We offer this book as a gentle pathway to reduce anxiety and fear and make your life's journey smoother, easier, and more joyful. All in the angelic realm have been with you since the beginning of time, helping, loving, and serving your development.

We say unto you: God loves you without judgment. You are seen as perfect. You hold the essence of God whispering new and wondrous ideas for you to bring forth into your physical world.

We urge you to take notes.

While you are reading our book, we greatly encourage you to take notes of additional questions and thoughts. If they are not answered within this book, we encourage you to send them to Rae for future books or through a private session with us. Rae no longer charges for these uplifting consultations.

We suggest you record the results of your daily decisions and choices as if you were a scientist in a laboratory. This will speed your journey to enlightenment. When you record the formulas you use to create the results you desire, you can more quickly discern what works and what does not.

Especially pay attention to the role your emotions play with each decision for they greatly affect the end results in creating either success or failure.

We will speak often throughout this book of the influence your emotions have upon your daily living and your seeking of happiness.

Imagine that God sent you on a mission to explore Earth. Become a scientist observing and experimenting and recording your results. You cannot fail in this endeavor. Your job is to bring forth new ideas and observe how they give you either positive or negative results. A scientist does not judge the results. A scientist only observes and records and experiments again gaining knowledge with each endeavor.

In other words, while you meditate within your quiet space, imagine yourself within your technical laboratory of physical experiments and record the knowledge you have gained from each. This record will prevent you from repeating the same formula of failure before you obtain your desired results.

The biggest detriment to your success is self-condemnation for what you deem to be poor decision-making. All life is simply another experiment in your soul's laboratory. Document the information, study the parts that worked and those that did not—and experiment again.

You will receive a bonus from your written words: we will use this communication to connect with you. Writing puts you into a semi-trance state. It is then we will whisper guidance and encouragement for you to follow your soul's plan. We will also send people who will help you along your path.

Over many lifetimes, you have explored belief systems generated from parents, teachers, and spiritual leaders. In this life, you may find yourself questioning them.

In creating your scientific journal, we encourage you to question anything we say that does not feel right or comfortable for you. Do not take our words as gospel. It is right and good for you to question. Still we ask that you hold off judgment until you have finished reading our book. Perhaps with a fuller understanding of our concepts and point of view, you will see your world from a different perspective.

More importantly, at the end of this book, your documentation of questions and observations in finding answers to all your long-held questions will become a channel to connect you with your angels and guides. May this book free you to spread your wings and fly.

Chapter 1
Who am I?

We say unto you, beloved soul:

God is Pure Love Energy

Giving life to all that exists in both

Physical and non-physical worlds.

God created your Soul

And sent it forth as an

Explorer to **Planet Earth**

within a perfect spacesuit called a

Physical Body

accompanied by a faster vibrating

duplicate body called a

Spirit

that holds your

Conscious Awareness

as well as all your

Emotions

that cannot reason or understand

but can trigger your

Mind and Heart

to rediscover that you are

One with God

Wow! That about sums it all up, Raphael!

Indeed, Rae, we have summarized the heart of all questions. And each one brings an answer that in turn brings you closer to God and the knowledge that we are all One with the Creator. Although we may oversimplify with the above statements, we shall elaborate further throughout this book so as to bring clarity to these concepts. Let these truths light your way through Earth's darkness and seeming loneliness. Know we are always with you, loving you and guiding you.

It's hard for us humans to comprehend what we cannot see, touch or feel. Even when we hear your voice within us, we question that it may be just our imagination. And then we can feel so alone.

God intended for Its beloved creations to be happy. Your emotions will tell you what truth is and what it is not. We encourage you to make a conscious choice to react to life's puzzles out of a sense of joyfulness rather than anxiety or fear. Only then shall you create beauty and goodness in solving every concern.

Our emotions are all over the place. How can we always be happy?

You cannot. You live within a planet with polarities. You will always experience both positive and negative emotions. The trick is to become aware of which end of the pendulum you are experiencing and then to choose how you will respond to balance your emotions and your life. When you release fear and anxiety and seek inner peace and divine love, you automatically raise your consciousness enough to contact God's angelic messengers. They can then assist you along your journey into the discoveries of your physical world.

But the question everyone wants to know is: **"Who or what is God?"**

We say unto you: **God is the Source of all energy**. All that exists is the vibrating energy supplied by the Source.

Now, that's something to ponder and I have come to believe this with all my heart and soul.
When I met my husband Bill (not his real name) and he told me he didn't believe in God, I thought, "Well this won't last long." But when I explained how I believed God was the energy by which everything exists, he thought a moment and said, "Then God is like this big generator in the sky and we all have extension cords plugged into Him?"
I laughed with delight and thought it was a wonderful visual.

Indeed it is. We shall not attempt to accurately describe or understand how one Mind can contain and hold constant awareness of all that exists in both physical and non-physical worlds. But God is always aware of ITSELF...*and you.*
Think of yourself as a vessel holding the God energy within your soul within your human body. It is the energy by which you

exist and breath and have your being. You are powerfully and exquisitely created to do what only you can do. You reflect divine energy that displays Itself as light. Therefore, we call you **a light being, a lamplighter** bringing forth God's light and love within your world.

When you first connected with me, I had never even heard of channeling and thus fear overwhelmed me. But with the encouragement of my friend, Landi who had witnessed channelers, I was able to dip my foot back into the waters of trans-channeling which is the term used when another entity can trade places with your spirit and use your body to express other-worldly ideas.

I had so much to learn about the whole idea, but Landi had just happened *to come to stay with me while she decided if she wanted to continue in her marriage or not. We did not know how life-changing her visit would be.*

We did know and had encouraged the visit through ideas whispered in your friend's ear.

And once we realized what was happening, we recorded the sessions with you, Raphael…and it again just happened *that my friend had two (not one, but* two*) transcribers whereby we could both listen to the cassettes and type the words into our computers.*

There are no coincidences, Rae. We had whispered to your friend to bring them. She had no idea why but did so anyway.

I am in awe of how angels work with us. I am also afraid I cannot ever measure up to the work you have set before me. I often feel so inadequate.

This is precisely why we have urged you to write this book, to channel our voice within you, to put aside doubt and anxiety that you are not perfect. No human is. But your willing heart is perfect, Rae. Be at peace and trust we will bring this knowledge forth for the greater good of all who read our words. We shall bring forth answers to the many questions asked so as to bring peace, harmony, and wisdom to all human souls upon your planet. We desire to make these complex subjects of who God is and who you are and why you are here joyfully acceptable to people of all faiths and beliefs with or without religious ties. We see the eternal search for Something or Someone greater than yourself. This search is inevitable as part of your soul's development within the physical world.

We have brought God's wisdom through many channelers throughout the centuries. They have been called saints or wise teachers of esoteric knowledge. For many of you, what we speak of here is not new knowledge. Yet, we present this material as if it were new. We desire only to uplift and inspire you, dear reader for your greatest good and happiness.

In God's infinite wisdom, it designed Its human creations to become co-creators with It. It sent forth souls to explore the denser energy of physical worlds.

Worlds? Plural?

Indeed, God is not limited as humans are. Many planets through many universes are inhabited by sentient beings.

I guess it is rather arrogant and naive of us to believe otherwise. But then again, most humans believe God is created in their image and likeness. They see God as a human man with a long white beard, sitting on a throne pointing where souls will go—either to heaven or to hell.

We say unto you...there is never any judgement from God and Its angels. A God of pure love energy could not create your visions of a fiery hell. There is only a heaven in which there are many dwelling places to suit each soul's needs and desires. Your master teacher, Jesus the Christ said how in his Father's house there were many mansions. Heaven is a faster vibrating dimension just beyond your earth's gravity. It has no polarities and thus is only filled with positive, loving energy. And indeed, it does have many mansions–dimensions of vibrational energy that match the vibration of each soul's stage of development. Beginner souls will be more comfortable with souls of like mind. Likewise advanced souls will find other advanced souls with whom to communicate.

Is that why when people return from a near-death experience, they say they didn't want to come back?

Indeed, this is so, for when your physical body dies, your spirit ascends into the perfect dimension to be compatible with their spiritual development. It is why all will call it Heaven.

But let's talk about how we came here in the first place. Explain how I got here, please.

The Process of Incarnation

Your coming to Earth required great preparation. First, God prepared your planet to inhabit sentient life. This alone took eons of your Earth development through your concept of time.

Then It designed and created your physical vehicle which has also evolved over eons of time.

I rather of imagine our bodies as an amazing space suit that God created for us so we could survive within the atmosphere of our planet.

It, too, has evolved to become what you are today.

So...can souls just decide they want to come to Earth and pop in?

No. There is a long preparation for a soul to be permitted to become an explorer of any planet. Your soul had to commit to a complete cycle of incarnations.

And what's a "cycle?" How long is it?

It cannot be measured in Earth's time. It differs with each soul and depends upon how quickly the soul absorbs the knowledge of manifestation. The beginning experiences are usually devoted to the soul adjusting to wearing a physical body. The soul's attention is totally focused on the body's pains and pleasures and thus you will observe sexual deviants and crimes related to physical pleasures. In order to grow from a beginner's perspective to that of an experienced explorer, the soul must go through many stages similar to a human child's development before becoming a successful productive adult.

Wow! Then are you saying that these baby souls are the ones creating all the havoc on our planet?

We will go into more detail about the stages of soul development which will reveal much about why people do what they do. For now, just know that souls evolve from its beginning stages of awareness to the advanced stage which requires many life experiences. Thus the need for a commitment to the entire cycle of lifetimes that will lead to adulthood and enlightenment. Exploration of your planet gains you mastery over the art of transforming non-physical matter such as a thought or a desire into dense matter such as a chair or a work of art.

So, we are learning how to become a Master of manifestation, turning God's ideas into something we can see or touch or feel.

Yes. And this takes many life experiences to master. Only a few souls come here already a master of the concepts in merging with the God Source. They are called Avatars.

Your Personal Guardian Angel

In preparing you for sentient life God appointed a personal angel to guide you throughout each life's exploration of your planet.

People often ask us how they can contact their guardian angel.

You can contact your angel by paying attention to your dreams and your daydreams with the inspirations to create beauty and goodness in your world.

But how do we hear our Guardian Angel?

You do not always hear a voice speaking from within. Angels speak the language of imagery and joy. You cannot hear them when you are within a dark emotional energy. You need to raise up your energy into a place of peace, harmony and joy to be able to hear our voices.

Oh! Well...please tell us how we do that.

Patience, dear Rae. We know you speak also for our readers. There are so many questions. One by one we shall try to answer them all.

Your *personal angel* is aware of your soul's purpose for your life. Imagine your Earth as a stage such as your Shakespeare suggested long ago. Your angel acts like your backstage manager and cue-master knowing the appropriate time to send forth new actors onto your Earth's stage.

Like when we say, "Something told me to..."

Indeed, your angel sends you flashes of pictures or abstract thoughts and ideas.

Like when you're thinking about someone and you picture them in your mind and suddenly they call you?

Yes, exactly. We say again, dear reader: <u>you are always within the heart and mind of God</u>. The Creator gently and lovingly looks after your every moment and breath ever since your conception within the mind of God. You have been given many gifts to accompany you on your journey through the physical. Your soul can create whatever God inspires of you. Rejoice in this.

Your Council of Elders

To guide you through your cycle of incarnations, God assigned your soul to a *Council of Elders* who are made up of master souls who no longer incarnate within a physical dimension. They act as your teachers and guides helping you plan each life before it begins, working with you throughout the life and reviewing it afterward. They guide you from the moment of your birth as a soul from the Source until your return to the soul world after each exploration of your physical world.

But it seems like too many people don't listen to their angel or Council's guidance.

This is because you have the gift of free will. God would not interfere with your freedom of choice for it is the means by which you explore new ideas and new emotional adventures. It is imperative that you experience both polarities of your planet. This means you will choose what you label as evil at some time or another. How else will your soul gather knowledge of your planet?

Some people may believe the Covid-19 is a punishment for our sins. Does God send these plagues to punish us?

Indeed not. God is pure love energy. Your planet is experiencing its own method of cleansing.

We speak of our planet as Mother Earth. Is she a live being ensouled within our planet?

Yes. This large evolved soul is trying to balance its body by throwing off pollutants like a shaggy dog shaking to throw off water. Thus, you have volcanic eruptions, earthquakes, tsunamis, tornadoes, hurricanes and plagues.

Is this because of how badly we have polluted our planet?

Indeed, pollution is choking Mother Earth and making her ill.

We noticed how during the lockdown because of this virus, people in very polluted countries were amazed to see clear skies like they had not seen in years. And yet some people refuse to acknowledge that we need to find a solution to global warming.

This is why some people believe this is the worst of times on our planet not only with global warming but because of great discord among nations and now with this pandemic.

Can you tell us more about this coronavirus? Are we really going to see the end of it soon?

The word corona refers to the halo around the virus. Unfortunately, those who discontinue the safeguards of personal distancing and extreme hygiene before the plague has died will experience a resurgence of the virus. It is a stubborn virus and will fight to stay alive. Only your scientists who seek a real inoculation can truly stop its spread. Again, this process needs real scientific trials that take time. There is no quick cure to this virus.

Plagues have swept across your planet in waves like tsunamis. It is a natural part of the makeup of your physical world, just as are earthquakes and volcanic eruptions. In the past, entire civilizations have been erased from your planet. You seek to blame it on some specific occurrence or some evil committed by a group. This is never the case. Some viruses, like this one came about when humans sold the flesh of wild animals for food that carried the virus to humans. It found the human species a great breeding factory and leapfrogged from one human to another eventually weakening the immune system and destroying the lungs. Scientists will always seek to find the cause to gain knowledge in the hopes of preventing it from recurring.

How is it some people seem to have a natural immunity to the virus?

This reflects the Divine Plan for each soul's story while on Earth's Stage.

But I've seen people arrogantly refusing to obey the precautions like social distancing and the wearing of masks and gloves. They declare they would never get it.

And they could be right—but there will be others who will be humbled when they contract the virus. This will in turn awaken others of like mind.

All of these seeming tragedies are but a human perspective as to the survival of humans. There are many factors within your planet's life that bring about such disasters.

Of course, knowledge gained from such experiences should teach us not to build a home at the base of a live volcano, but we never seem to learn. People build homes on cliffs that are known to disappear in mudslides. They continue to build on coastal waters where tsunamis are known to make entire cities disappear.

Wise souls do learn and try to teach others how to prepare. And yet beginner souls in government in their grab for power may contradict the wisdom of their elders.

We have seen this in our government's handling of the Coronavirus. Like a child who wants to go outside and play while a tornado is rampaging, we are given mixed messages as to when the tornado will "just disappear."

We understand how inexperienced souls seek their own pleasures. Long ago, we predicted this time of confusion and discord among humans over global warming. We saw how the raising of consciousness would begin when there was transparency within your political scenes throughout the world, when lies become known as lies, and fact-checking would reveal truth. One could no longer hide behind a smile that holds false intent. Thousands will awaken to a higher sense of integrity, honesty, compassion, and love. They will rise up and demand truth. It is the beginning of a new awareness that you are all one within God.

And so, dear reader, we shall put forth these thoughts and ideas into a new understanding of why you came to Earth. For some it is because we have called you to join us like a lamp in the darkness. And yet you may feel as if you are still in darkness. We come to lead you into joy to experience inner peace and harmony and thus share this new awakening with many other souls as well.

During this time, you will discover the bliss of knowing who and what God is as you feel Its divine energy of love and peace within you. You will glow with the light of God such that others will become inspired when basking in your bliss. When you shine brightly, you ignite the hearts of all around you and they too, become God's Lamplighters. Their light inspires others to become Lamplighters and so on until this chain reaction changes your world and God is made manifest within your world.

It is now this Time of Times. Rejoice in it.

Rejoice that your species has come a long way from its beginnings.

Therefore, we say unto you: explore your planet, test out your ideas, learn through trial and error, and know that nothing you do is ever judged by God as evil or even as good or better than another. The Creator sees you as perfect and delights in you just as you are in each moment in time.

We need to summarize this chapter with one question: Who and What is God? And Who and What Am I?

God is the divine energy by which everyone and everything exists. Therefore, God knows you intimately as It is the breath through which you breathe. It is the mind through which you connect with Itself and with one another.

God is pure love. It cannot conceive of creating discord or evil. It did not create a purgatory or a hell. Only humans within a planet of polarities can experience good and evil—your terms to describe energy as it flows through you and your environment colored by the dense nature of Earth. Be not deceived: There is no Devil. There is only your planet's pull on your emotions to explore its dense negative polarity. It is well and good for your soul to reap what it has sown, for only in so doing can you discern and define your emotional and physical reaction to each experience.

What is Evil and are there really devils?

The Between World

There are souls whose life experience was steeped in the negative pole of your planet, expressed by lack of integrity, and excess of greed and dishonesty that can even lead to the taking of another's life for personal gain. When they die, they can become stuck between your earth's vibration and the joyous vibration of what you call heaven.

It is from this Between World that these souls try to continue their life upon your planet by influencing souls of like mind to follow their desires and the aborted plans for their life. These dark entities have lost their connection with their soul that is pure and desiring to do the work of God's light and wisdom.

This is why we again urge you to record your experiences and ask our guidance in helping you reap all the knowledge and wisdom you can from them.

Know this: every experience becomes the fruit of wisdom, for it is the way of your world. Do not judge yourself or others.

In the next chapter, Raphael will describe how each of us is uniquely and perfectly designed to be God's explorers within our physical world.

Chapter 2
What is a Soul?

Following your first description of who God is and who you are leads us to describe what a soul is and what it looks like. During each personal reading, Raphael shows me a visual of each soul as a brilliant sunbeam filled with what looks like Fourth of July sparklers all dancing in its own DNA pattern and emanating vibrant color and celestial music.

Indeed, souls are truly magnificent! Your soul is made up of a specific vibration of color revealing its purpose and point of view. This vibration never changes. The soul's size can change with the accumulation of knowledge gained from your soul's physical experiences.

I laughed when you told me this and thought, "It's better to be a fat soul than a skinny one!" So, a soul actually expands with new knowledge gained from each incarnation?

Yes. A soul grows in size just as a human grows from a tiny baby to a full-gown adult. You may compare each incarnation of the soul to each birthday of a human.

Does that mean we could have a hundred lives?

And more. Some souls love telling their stories on Earth's stage. Others cannot wait to be done with it.

Your soul came forth from one of God's seven rays to co-create with It while exploring physical worlds. We shall elaborate further on this later, but for now, let us speak of another part of you that is equally important...

Your Spirit Body

God placed a small portion of your soul's vibrating energy within your **physical vehicle of expression.** You become God's eyes, ears, arms and legs to explore in detail all of Its creations within your planet.

This portion of your soul's energy merged within your new physical being. We call it your **spirit consciousness**.

And if people saw it, they would call it a ghost.

Some gifted people can see spirits who have passed and can communicate with them. You call them mediums.

I loved the series called, "Ghost Whisperer." It showed a young woman who was able to see and speak with spirits who were stuck in Earth's dimension—the Between World. These ghosts tried to speak to their loved ones but no one could see or hear them.

Your spirit receives divine thoughts and ideas and translates them into human experiences. It learns balance while amidst the push and pull between the dark energy of your planet with the energy of light. In beginning lifetimes the soul does not know how to connect with its spirit self, thus causing it to feel abandoned and alone. But as a soul advances in divine wisdom, it can more easily communicate with its spirit partner.

We say again: God created your soul to be an explorer of physical worlds. The more knowledge you gain from each experience, the better you are at making decisions bearing fruit rather than disappointment.

Begin with the knowledge that you, dear reader, are most likely an experienced soul, otherwise you would not have chosen to read this book.

God's Rainbow of Souls and Its Stages of Development

When you explained the development of a soul's conscience, it helped me understand why people do the terrible things they do. Then, when you explained how beginner souls are like babies who are only interested in experiencing the physical pleasures of the body…well, it all began to make sense.

Anything that enters the physical world takes on solid form vibrating to its own unique energy and radiating color and sound. Souls are pure spirit made up of vibrating energy birthed through one of God's seven energy rays that define the soul's personality and perspective on life. They create a splendid display of lights upon your planet.

Your soul sparkles with a brilliance never to be overcome by darkness. A soul's celestial song may be heard by advanced souls while in their human form.

Are the tuning forks and crystal bowls and metal gongs people have created for healing anywhere close to the vibrational sound of souls?

Oh, yes. This energy as expressed in sound is very healing for the physical body. And yet souls vibrate many, many octaves higher than the human body. You need to understand each soul's uniqueness. No two souls—even twins in human form have different souls, which is why they can look alike but be so different.

I know a woman whose twin is entirely different from her. You helped her understand that the twin had to be coaxed to return to Earth to overcome her addiction to alcohol. She would not return until the woman agreed to let her tag along as a twin. And yet the woman is addicted to alcohol once again.

We will talk about addictions later, but this scenario is not uncommon.

You need to speak of a soul's purpose and point of view as well as their developing maturity. This was the most revealing information you gave me that helped me have a greater patience and compassion for my fellow humans.

To further help you understand the variety and expanse of a soul's perspective of life on your planet, we will begin with describing their frequency vibration by comparing the sound of the tuning fork's resonance.

Is there any connection to a soul's experiences to having experienced a variety of races? And if so, how does it influence a soul's particular experience of the life and their response to life?

Although that is a limited viewpoint, we can see how you would use it as an example of a soul's point of view. But we say unto you, each soul will choose to experience each race before it has completed its study of being a sentient being on your physical Earth. The racial influences, the reaction of other races to one another and the prejudices and privileges that accompany those experiences are all part of the soul's study of being a human within your Earth.

So...those who are prejudiced against a specific race...will they return in that race in another lifetime?

You are beginning to grasp why it takes so many lifetimes before a soul advances into non-judgment, compassion and love for all humankind.

Oh yeah. But then again, it makes it easier to identify those mature souls who hold no prejudices, who have a great deal of compassion for others, and who seem to always express inner peace.

Indeed, Rae, this is so. Advanced souls who have experienced a lifetime of racial discrimination against them, will no longer express prejudice, but instead will defend the defenseless and fight for equality.

So please, Raphael, give us detailed descriptions of each soul's vibration and color and how we can identify them. Maybe it will help us to be less judgmental.

The Development of Soul Personalities

The Red-Ray Soul's purpose is to develop leadership. It vibrates to your tuning fork's sound of C which resonates at 256 Hz. The red soul needs to be grounded in earth's energy so as to focus on practical and earthly things.

This soul's challenges are expressed through acts of courage and leadership. It desires to be in charge and in the beginning lifetimes may become a tyrant, demanding loyalty or death.

A red soul's energy will vibrate in red throughout its entire existence. A soul never changes its vibrational color.

The Orange-Ray Soul vibrates to the tuning fork's sound of D. It, too, is well grounded. God sends only a very few of these souls into the planet at one time. They are often tide changers of spiritual energy, bringing forth new perceptions of God.

These souls often become a leader of souls rather than of armies. They come in with advanced knowledge and spiritual wisdom and hold a close connection to the Creator. They become bearers of a profound message to multitudes of souls which may start a movement or a religion. They usually begin as an advanced soul and do not have to go through all the stages of soul growth. Since these souls enter the planet as an advanced soul, there are very few on the planet at any given time.

The Yellow-Ray Soul's energy vibrates to the frequency of the tuning fork E. It focuses on the mind and intellect leading them toward research and study. These souls may become the architects, mathematicians, and scientists of the world. They have keen minds and can be considered geniuses. Some savants are yellow souls who delight in spouting facts that flabbergast others.

The Green-Ray Soul vibrates to the energy of F on the scale. It is a balance between the three slower vibrating energies of red, orange and yellow and the faster soul vibrations of blue, indigo and violet. This soul seeks to be of service to others, to heal and to help in any way presented.

The Blue-Ray Soul vibrates to G and radiates a light-blue color. This soul is often multi-talented, expressing abstract ideas in many different creative roles such as teacher, inspirational speaker, musician, actor, writer, and so forth.

The Indigo-Ray Soul vibrates to the A tuning fork as the deep bluish/purple of an indigo color. It is the vibration used for tuning an orchestra of 440 Hz.

People with this soul energy are often labeled strange. They like being different. Because of their ability to think out-of-the-box, these souls tend to imagine possible future scenarios and prepare for them or even seek to create them, thus making them inventors of unusual projects.

The Violet-Ray Soul vibrates at the fastest frequency of all soul vibrations to the B tuning fork. (Please remember faster/slower; higher/lower has no connotation as to good, better or best).

These souls resonate with a violet or purple color. It is focused on other-worldly information, desiring to gain understanding of God and the afterlife.

Chapter 3
Why Do People Do Terrible Things to One Another?

Dear souls: We say unto you it is because they do not know what they do.

And it is because souls have growing pains!

Souls are always coming and going within your planet in varying stages of soul development from a baby to an adult.

Some come into the physical without having had any previous experience in exploring your world. Their spirits have a wide-eyed curiosity along with total ignorance of your rules, laws and niceties as defined by more advanced souls who have set up those laws and regulations. New souls often discover those laws often by breaking them and reaping the consequences.

An Overview of a Soul's Stages of Growth

New souls may seem to be of lesser mental abilities for their minds are a clean slate. And yet, they could be a genius awakening to new ideas from God because there is no obstruction of preconceived ideas to block the communication with their Creator. Their abilities for problem-solving may astound others. It is because they do not have past experiences of failure that close them off from our inspirations.

Just as humans grow from infancy to toddlers who put everything into their mouths in exploring their world, so does a soul's spirit consciousness when it first inhabits a sentient being as they begin their coursework of becoming co-creators with God.

Beginner Souls

In the beginning, the soul's spirit is consumed with the need to learn how to maneuver in comfort within its new body containing a mind and emotions. Survival becomes the first and all-consuming thought. It will taste fear for the first time. Fear can lead to paranoia that can lead to extreme actions of self-protection.

These new spirits have no conscience and will try anything and everything for its physical body's comfort. Although they may have parents who try to teach them the consequences of actions, it is only through first-hand experience, through trial and error that the beginner soul with its newly formed spirit can learn. Thus beginner souls may commit many sins against their fellow humans.

Beginner spirits often have very short lives.

Souls in the Intermediate Stage

After many lifetimes of exploring your planet, after many more births, deaths and life-reviews are added to the soul's book of physical adventures, the soul enters the next level of development that we shall call the Intermediate Stage.

By this time, the soul will have gained experience in learning to express its needs more humanely and yet still selfishly. It has learned many methods of persuasion but may still manipulate, coerce or cheat another. It learns how to use language to negotiate, to barter and trade, but still finds devious ways to reach its desired objectives. These young souls will seem to seek justice as they set up a selection of judges to rule the laws they will put into place often to suit their own needs.

Most souls on your planet right now are in this stage from the beginning of it where they may still seem like newly minted souls up to the latter part of this stage when finally these souls seem to accept the rules of sentient life.

Souls in the Advanced Stage of Growth

After many, many more lifetimes, souls will have learned that it is better to give than to receive. They will become conscious they are "we" rather than "I." In the beginning of this stage, they may become over scrupulous in their desire to do "good." They will show compassion for all races including the stranger and the thief. They will have an obsessive desire to find God and experience inner peace. They shed their desire to acquire the riches of your planet. Many of you who read this book are at this mature level of human development. You are well on your way to becoming an enlightened human being.

Individual Development of Each Soul's Vibration

Red Souls

Beginner Red Souls are often tyrants demanding you do things their way or it is off with your head! They demand loyalty and admiration. They can have temper tantrums exacting punishment for disobedience or disloyalty. Red souls often choose a masculine body with strength and muscle so as to have control over others. And yet when the soul discovers they have a less-than-perfect body, they may use even more control over others to make up for it.

Intermediate Red Souls have gained experience through many lifetimes of force versus power to understand they are two very different things. They will still crave power and control over others believing that is the only way to be in control and may still use unethical means to obtain that power. Their conscience and ethics are still lacking. They make great con artists and may become involved in large mob-like organizations, seeking to climb that type of corporate ladder.

An Advanced Red Soul will in the beginning stages of this part of their soul's development have had enough lifetimes to learn the consequences of their actions and yet, past lives of defrauding people may pull at them. They remember it fondly. To be a corporal in an army leading his troops to victory still has fond memories. But when lifetimes of experience build, they will now choose to become a humanitarian and give back what they have learned. Many who were once considered evil leaders in the destruction of many, will at this stage become a philanthropic leader who can benefit millions. With a raised consciousness they can become a wise benevolent leader.

Orange Souls

Orange Souls usually enter as advanced souls. They come as avatars and enlightened beings. There are only a very few on your planet at one time. You may recognize them by their wisdom and gentle disposition showing love and compassion for all humanity. They are often known only to a few as they do not seek public approval.

Yellow Souls

Beginner Yellow Souls love to tinker and play with ideas and never want to grow up. They will invent just for the fun of it. They may invent some wonderful new machine that they will simply let sit in their garage, for they do not see value in it. Others may seek to exploit their innocence.

Many yellow souls are child geniuses with an amazing knowledge of mathematics or science or the arts. They often become exploited by others for their abilities.

Intermediate Yellow Souls seek to discover a miracle drug or some invention so as to gain fame and fortune for their efforts. They are not above using other people's ideas and claiming them as their own. An inner sense of right versus wrong has not developed enough for them to show anything other than their own selfish needs.

While yellow souls are often centered on their intellect, their emotions can range from child-like temper tantrums to wise old souls. They can be very forceful in gaining their way in expressing life.

Advanced Yellow Souls may work tirelessly to create a cure for some disease or an invention for the advancement of the greater good. Yet one can be an advanced yellow soul and not give away all that he/she has discovered but may demand an equal share in the advancement of the work to share with the world. Patents are often required with credits given.

Green Souls

Beginner Green Souls often find themselves becoming slaves to others who learn to expect their help without regard for the needs of this soul. And so a self-sacrificing expectation can become their catch 22. Souls in this energy may seek jobs as healers, clerks, secretaries or administrative assistants.

Because this soul's energy is among the majority of souls along with the red soul energy upon your planet, they do tend to balance one another.

Green souls always make good partners within personal or work relationships because they will seek the greatest good for all concerned even if they are the newest of green souls.

Intermediate Green Souls may often become the slave of another's obsessions. They still seek to find a mate who will take care of them, love them unconditionally and make them happy. They are too often disappointed in love as they become a slave in the expectation to fill the needs of a partner.

Green souls often take on female bodies because of their desire to serve and may seek roles as nurses, social workers, doctors, therapists, salesclerks, bookkeepers, nannies, or waiters. They will seek any profession where they can help others. Green-soul men are now entering these professions as they seek to find a role that will benefit humanity.

We often find many green souls among the male LGBTQ communities as they are raising the consciousness of the world in showing it is okay to be a male showing compassion for others, to take on women's roles and do them well. This movement is bringing balance among the sexes and contrary to the conflicting beliefs of others, has brought much good to your world.

Advanced souls of the green ray dedicate their lives to helping others by selecting professions within the medical world or in counseling or in being of service in any way. They often become leaders in the movement for equal rights, for defending the innocent, for bringing forth new laws that will stop exploitation of others, of helping children or the homeless or any form of injustice within their world.

Blue Souls

A beginner Blue Soul may seem very childlike and innocent, expressing itself in the arts with an unusual gift. It creates for the joy of creating not for fame or fortune. They can be exploited by others. It does not matter to this child-like soul. They will often express humor and tolerance beyond the understanding of their elders. And yet, this beginner soul will see life simply as good or evil. They can be quite paranoid once they discover "evil," and as they grow into adults will seek to express themselves as leaders of truth according to a set of rules they choose to follow.

Intermediate Blue Souls will thrive on an audience, living for the applause. They will work diligently to improve their gifts so as to be better at their trade as artists, actors, screen writers, etc. They often live a drama-filled life with many interpersonal relationships that disrupt and upset their concept of a good life. They may feel misunderstood and abused in every which way. They can become very verbal in expressing their displeasures through the written word or even from the pulpit. They may rewrite the bible according to their inspired interpretation and have many followers of their newly created religion.

Advanced Blue Souls begin to seek more than the applause. They question the purpose of life and often become involved in seeking those who are of advanced spiritual knowledge. They may choose to study all religions just to understand their fellow human's perspective. They become tolerant of all points of view. They are often spiritually motivated in all their endeavors. But they do not seek fame or fortune, only new knowledge. They may be a leader of small study groups who also seek advanced spiritual knowledge.

As their creative energies expand and they often show great talent beyond what they had previously displayed. They will want to share their new experiences in written form or even in creating workshops to teach others their hard-earned wisdom.

Indigo Souls

A beginner Indigo Soul may feel overwhelmed with the push and pull of creating versus stagnation and self-doubt. It will work on new ideas in bursts and stops. It will display great wisdom intuitively and will want to rescue the world from itself. They can become "seers" or "psychics" who work for a profit, even defrauding people using scare tactics like removing a bad spirit—for a fee. They can be so-called friends who are busy bodies who want to help you with their superior knowledge and wisdom. They want you to follow their visions and can be forceful in their endeavor to influence others to their way of thinking.

An intermediate Indigo Soul may still feel overwhelmed with the confusion of its purpose in life. It may seek many occupations to discover its place in the world. It is constantly filled with new ideas but does not feel adequate to bring forth into reality. Much beauty and creativity come from this stage. They often are leaders in the fields of education or in the corporate world because of their ability to accurately project future possibilities. But again, in this stage, their motives may not always be for the greater good.

An advanced Indigo soul will likely find its niche early in life and simply expand upon it. It will tend toward the arts and bring forth many creative ideas that it shares with others without needing credit for it. They avoid all labels and instead lead quiet lives that still attract others to seek their guidance and wisdom. These indigo souls do not seek fame or financial rewards. They will always be helping in raising consciousness.

The Indigo soul is often unique in their personal appearance, enjoying bold colors and designs or hair styles. They can be fluid and open-minded in their problem solving. They often have several projects going at one time.

Violet Souls

Beginner Violet-Ray Souls may see spirits and react in fear rather than acceptance or trust. Many may demonstrate extra sensory perception. As with any beginner soul, they tend toward more fear and anxiety than trust and love. Beginner violet souls focus on other worlds. They seem to be dreamers and visionaries. They are often quite psychic.

In the **middle stages,** the violet soul may want to be an evangelist to save people from their projected vision of a colorful fiery hell. They will display the motivation of desiring fame and fortune, which can lead them down a path of destruction when they put money and power before God. The souls from this ray will eventually display confusion about what they believe and begin to question everything.

Toward the end of this stage, these souls may give up all belief systems, claiming they no longer hold strong beliefs or dogma and may claim to be agnostics and atheists. This conclusion is of course not limited to violet souls. Many who question their beliefs may swing the pendulum toward disbelief in an afterlife or of God before some profound experience swings them back so quickly they may feel the whiplash! Near-death experiences are the wake-up call when the person actually goes to the next dimension and sees for themselves what glory awaits them after death.

Advanced souls of this perspective become filled with tolerance, compassion, and love for their fellow humans. They do not condemn or judge, but stress God's unconditional love for all people and their desire to bring God's presence to others. They seem to glow from the inside out. They are always smiling, finding good in everything, and seem to exude a joy of living and an appreciation for the gift of life.

The above gives me a brief and yet complex understanding of why God created Reincarnation. Many view this concept of many lives with raised eyebrows either because it goes against their religious beliefs or because they cannot conceive of enduring another life like what they are presently experiencing.

We would offer a different perspective of reincarnation. Imagine you are a famous author of hundreds of books that are all best sellers. You love writing stories. Would it not be a thrill if all your stories were immediately turned into a movie where you are the director, the producer, **and** the leading actor? Would it not be a thrill to have your movie win an Oscar?

This is your soul—the author of each lifetime's story. This negates the belief that souls do not wish to return to sentient life. They **love** writing stories to act out on Earth's stage. There is a waiting list of souls wanting to tell their stories.

Because your soul does not experience emotions as you do as its human partner, it can throw in all kinds of emotional challenges and observe how you, the leading character responds within the thick energy of a physical dimension. This then allows your soul to alter the story to always make you the hero/heroine who overcomes all difficulties.

From a sentient being's perspective, you may not wish to return to Earth when your life has been a challenge. It is not so with your soul. As soon as the lifetime is over and after your spirit has completed its life review and gone on to its experience of Heaven, the soul returns home and discusses its story with its soul mates.

Soul mates????

Ah yes...soul mates. We do not speak of lovers here. We hear your questions and we will speak of love relationships later.

We speak of your soul group as your soul friends who are of the same vibrational color and stage of development as you are. Your classmates have been together throughout many lifetimes and enjoy trading stories. You have a mentor, sometimes someone from your Council, which you all share. It helps you gain as much new knowledge from each life experience as possible. There is much serious discussion as well as delightful laughter during these sessions. Your soul is fully detached from the emotional element of your life and can speak freely of the life experience as if it were a story on a movie screen. In fact, your guide can call up specific scenes at will, for all of your lives are recorded in your book of life, which is stored in the Hall of Knowledge in yet another dimension.

For now we speak of your soul who studies and learns with other souls of equal development and vibrational energy. Your soul's perspective is vastly different from your viewpoint as a sentient being.

Remember, your spirit body is specifically designed to be an exact duplicate of your physical body. It holds the consciousness of your soul but is separate from it. Your spirit continues to exist after death as it ascends into the world of spirit where it gathers more information for your soul who is constantly in contact with it.

After your soul has garnered all it can from your spirit's voyage into the spirit dimension, it will merge with your soul just as a human will merge a memory of a specific adventure within its beingness. Your unique character played by your spirit can be recalled as an exact memory of any life. When a medium calls forth a spirit, the soul releases information in its fullness not as a memory, but as an exact replay of that life. The soul has total recall of every moment of every life experience. It is like an actor who once he has learned a script can step into the part at any given time.

Souls who first incarnate upon your planet begin like a human infant with no knowledge of the rules of life within a physical body. Their main purpose is survival. They seek only comfort within their new body. Before they came they were made up of spirit energy free to move with only a thought. Now they have a physical body made up of 95% water sloshing around in a magnetically grounded, and extremely <u>heavy</u> bodysuit.

With each lifetime, the soul also endures the slow process of the physical body's growing pains from infant to adult. It learns to walk all over again by standing and falling many times. It learns to speak a new language while at the same time learning to control its bodily functions as well as adjust to a new environment of heat or cold or of safety or danger.

The returning soul has to learn to adjust to new parents and perhaps siblings—all who are usually souls from a previous lifetime. You may be balancing a previous life experience of abundance by experiencing poverty or visa-versa. Your soul sorts out new beliefs from new teachers. It puzzles to discern what is true and what is false, what is real and what is imagined.

It acquires an understanding of the new rules of the present environment.

Most importantly, your soul must learn to communicate to its human partner its plans for the life. That alone can be quite a task. Often beginner souls find their human is like a runaway horse with the bit in its teeth. All communication is lost. The soul just goes along for the ride, watching its carefully laid plans blowing in the wind.

This is what gives your soul growing pains. Sometimes when the soul has a breakthrough, you may call it Deja vu. You feel you have done this before, been there before.

The soul, like the human, uses trial and error, success and failure in this connection, getting better and better with each lifetime, advancing from an infant soul's perspective in the beginning life experiences to the wisdom of an adult soul where there is a joyous connection between soul and sentient being. We stress how we are speaking of a soul's understanding and wisdom regarding sentient life on a planet. Therefore, it is your soul's growing pains within each lifetime that advances it from one level to another. This can take many, many lifetimes.

While a soul never changes its vibrational energy or color, the accumulation of information and wisdom gathered from each lifetime's experiences does change the soul's size from a small beam of light to a large column of divine energy swelling with experience and divine love.

Although it is certain that your planet will survive, some believe it may be too late for your species to do so. They reason that it would not be the first group of sentient beings who became extinct.

Although the premise is true, we do not agree with the conclusion. Your species will survive its present challenges and become a super race, not of one color but of an entire mixture of blends that will allow it to gain the wisdom to use their energy only for the good of all and not for the few. We agree that this could take perhaps another fifty to one-hundred years.

Many Councils have deemed it necessary for those infant and baby souls who have been a destructive influence on humanity to be barred from returning to your planet to complete their incarnational cycle. After they complete their present life on Earth's stage, they will continue on another planet that has been prepared for them. Indeed, it is now inhabited. Your scientists have recently discovered it.

We encourage you to expand your consciousness to know that beyond your limited viewpoint, there are other worlds in your universe that are inhabited with various forms of sentient, ensouled beings. God is not limited in Its creative powers.

Many in the spiritual dimension are working with previous groups of souls who have brought enlightenment to your planet. We speak of those developed humans such as the Incas and early Native Americans who helped humankind to become aware of life beyond the physical and have left clues of how to save your species. New medicines come from old cures. The one called the "Sleeping Prophet" brought forth many old recipes for healing. Edgar Cayce was a simple man who could lie down and go to sleep and leave his body so as to allow other advanced souls to enter his physical form and give healing information. His readings have been documented in the Edgar Cayce Institute in Virginia Beach.

Many more enlightened souls have incarnated at this time of the planet's great need. They are reaching thousands of people with new ideas that open the mind to metaphysical facts and truths.

And still...only souls mature enough to be open to these new ideas will be able to receive them.

We remind you—all ideas, thoughts and visions resonate from the divine energy—God.

God has also sent angelic beings to incarnate within the human form. They do not go through the cycle of incarnations but incarnate as advanced souls. They may seem ethereal and otherworldly, exhibiting great light, peace and joy. Usually they do not have many followers but will train a few to go out and become inspirational speakers and leaders of advanced thinking. You can find many of them on your television program called *Ted Talks*. We encourage you to open your minds and hearts and souls to explore new ideas, to discover those who think out of the box, those who bring forth new challenges to the norm. These are the new way—showers—they are the true new wave or "Second Coming" of Christed beings.

Know this: there are never any failures in God's eyes. The art of free will is the art of experimentation. It requires the use of the human mind to try something new when the first idea did not work. While within the physical you must obey the physical laws of your world such as time, space, and gravity. An idea does not materialize instantly. Ideas build upon ideas until a physical reality takes shape.

Your Thomas Edison had hundreds of so-called failures before creating the light bulb. He did not see them as failures. He saw them as experimentations that led to success. All artists, inventors, and creative thinkers know how to use their minds to go into a light trance state where they can receive ideas from those in the higher realms. We will discuss this later in the book.

There are souls who have passed into the next realm who cooperate with such people who have learned to be open to new ideas. A skeptic cannot receive them without a great deal of doubt, research and study. A cynic cannot even begin to be open to it. This also reflects a soul's stage of development within physical worlds. It is all right to be skeptical and to fact-check what is claimed to be a fact. Humans often confuse emotional opinions as facts. A fact is a documentation of an idea through research by recreating an abstract idea to prove consistency in results. Only then is it considered a fact. By keeping a journal of your beliefs, you can prove a feeling or an emotional reaction such as anger to be triggered by certain actions of others or certain physical events to be a fact. But esoteric knowledge brought forth from ancient wisdom often cannot be turned into provable facts.

We say unto you, dear reader: It is through deep meditation or a light sleep state when God sends messengers who in their glorified bodies can telepathically project ideas to those still in physical bodies. We mean to say that those who have passed and have learned to communicate with the living will bring forth new ideas and new truths—of course, depending upon that entity's soul's wisdom at the time. Therefore, it behooves you not to accept the whispering of another who has passed what they deem as divine truth. It is only their truth as the development of that soul's knowledge deems wisdom. Be diligent in what is given by an entity who has passed and now comes forth to speak *truth* from the *beyond. Only discernment can bring to you truth and wisdom* as a projection of God's infinite knowledge like a seed ready for watering that becomes a beautiful creation in your world. Everyone and everything that exists in any physical or non-physical world is an expression of God. Only you label it as good, bad, or neutral.

There is a divine plan set forth for each soul's life and your council closely watches your every thought, word and deed. They continually inspire, uplift and encourage you toward success. God experiences your every breath for **IT is your life**

breath and vitality. You breathe in God's essence continuously and It continues to help you to expand and change and grow.

We cannot say this often enough: **you and God are one.**

We know this concept of oneness is difficult for an earth-bound being, but know it is so. Otherwise we would not say it is. Your scientists can testify that everything is made up of energy. We say again and again: **God is the divine energy by which everything and everyone exists.**

Perhaps this information on soul development will help you understand why mature and advanced souls working on your planet now can be the inspiration in saving your planet.

Be assured that the raising of consciousness is already happening. You have seen it in your women's movements to bring equality of the sexes. You have seen it in the transparency in your political scenes. You have seen it in the protestations all around the world of people uniting for freedom of thought, freedom of government, and freedom to earn enough in wages to live a comfortable life.

And yet this freedom can be misunderstood in those who demand their right to choose to ignore the warnings regarding the coronavirus that is presently rampaging throughout your planet. The prevention of the spread of the disease is not a choice but a sign of wisdom and compassion for others. Those who do not choose to wear masks are showing their soul's immaturity.

Without greed for power and financial rewards, many solutions to problems will be discovered and promoted by a greater number of people who have come to realize not only the importance for a cleaner environment, but also an uplifting of consciousness for saving your species. Enlightenment will diminish the corruption caused by a few seeking personal power without concern for the consequences to the many. It will bring about a resurgence of governments ruled by the people rather than by a powerful few.

Indeed, we repeat it is not too late for the survival of your species or for the healing of your planet. The seeds planted long ago are now sprouting with wiser and more humane leadership. Your world is changing for the better.

It is in your hands now as to how quickly this will manifest. Use your light as a voice for your planet. Do not hide your light under that biblical bushel basket. Know that the prophets of old spoke to a generation yet to come and their wisdom still holds divine truth. This does not mean to find a soap box and preach to others what they must do. Each soul will find its winding path to God. Rather it means for you to become God's Lamplighter by simply exhibiting integrity, compassion, kindness, humor, generosity and joy within your personal world. This will automatically inspire and spread to others.

Indeed, all of humanity is reaping what it has sown. Humans are presently experiencing the consequences of their experiments of stealing power from the masses to use for their own selfish interests. There is a new wave of positive energy that is raising human consciousness through concern for your planet now suffering from global warming. We predict that many will speak up to bring a new kind of peace that will strive to give power back to governments working for the benefit of all peoples, not just a few who seek wealth at the expense of the poor.

Be of good heart. We say unto you: this is now happening. We predicted this several years ago, suggesting it would become apparent when there was transparency within your world as is now available through your visual media. Fact checking was created when lies were presented as truth. Although distrust can be the first wave, it is the motivator to begin practicing discernment and responsibility for actions based on those facts, not on an emotional desire for what is not true to be true.

Chapter 4
What About My Physical Body?

With the help of your Council of Elders, your soul carefully designed your physical vehicle of expression within which it could act as the leading character in your Earth story. They carefully selected your parents and the pattern of your DNA, as well as your sexual, intellectual, and spiritual attributes.

When we share this information, some have become alarmed saying they would never have chosen the people who were their parents. We gently clarify that indeed they did <u>not</u> choose them. The soul with the aid of its Council chose your parents for a number of reasons. The role you play within each life drama has far greater meaning and purpose than you can ever imagine. Most often, you have played a role with your parents in another lifetime and you come back to enjoy the relationship one again or you come back to resolve conflicts that carried over into the present life.

Your human conscious mind has no part of this intricate pre-planning for it must begin the life with a clean slate. Only when it is seen to aid you in your spirit in its progress through the physical may you be given a peek of a previous lifetime—or even a peek of a lifetime to come. This is so you can focus on simply being able to survive and live a long life as well as gain new information along the way for your soul.

There are multiple interactions and responses between you and the people you will influence during your life upon the planet. You will not even be aware of this until you leave your world at the end of your life and go with your spirit into the next dimension. When you have your life review, you will only begin to see the bigger picture of your influence with others and their influence upon you.

Again, we say, all is one with the divine mind—God. This tapestry of human lives is woven by God in a glorious and intricate tapestry of energy colored with emotions and varying thought patterns. It is unimaginable in its magnificence. Yet it is a cloth in constant motion, constantly weaving with your thoughts, actions and reactions to each and every decision you make. Rejoice in this, beloved soul.

Your Council waited for the exact astrological moment for you to be born. During this waiting period, your soul observed your future birth family that included extended families on both parents' side.

Beginner souls do not have much say in this process, as they do not know enough about life in the physical dimension to do so. More experienced souls may have more input with their Council in setting up the story's outline and the list of characters they wish to involve within their story. The soul often calls upon soul friends to accompany them again to Earth.

Before birth, the embryo maintains life through the umbilical cord connecting it to the mother's energy. The soul's consciousness visits the tiny form, moving in and out as if testing its progress. We give you this information so that you can understand that a miscarriage or an abortion during this gestation period is not the murder of an ensouled being. We are sure this knowledge will not change your present laws or the beliefs of young souls, It is for you to know and understand that, again, God does not judge. God only gives Its divine energy freely for you to create whatever you desire with a passion and a determination to bring forth as your reality.

It is not until just before birth that the soul merges within the infant and then it is only a small portion of the soul's enormous energy that breathes consciousness into the physical body with its first breath outside the womb. This portion of the soul becomes an exact duplicate of the newly formed physical body and vibrates faster than the physical body making it invisible to the human eye. Clairvoyants can see this spirit form and may call it your ghost. This ghostly form survives your physical body after death and will transcend into the next dimension of the spirit world, which is a dimension that is not a place like your planet but is rather God's thought-form where spirits gather after the life experience has been completed. It is what you often call Heaven because it no longer has the pull of your

Earth's magnetic poles. Only positive energy resides there. And yet, you in your spirit form will feel it is another more perfect Earth. In this dimension, you will experience the ability to create whatever you desire almost instantly. It is an opportunity to practice the art of co-creating with God's energy that is always positive.

When I first read Dr. Raymond Moody's book, "Life After Life," I was amazed at his descriptions of people's near-death experiences. Many since have related such experiences—and all have had similarities, proving it is a fact, not the fiction of a traumatized mind. The joy the spirit experiences in the next dimension would make it difficult if you were asked to return to the chaos of the earth plane!

Birth

When you were born, your soul entered a portion of its energy that we call your spirit. It did so with your first breath to sustain life outside of the mother's womb. Sometimes beginner souls do not give enough of its energy to the newborn child and it can cause crib death.

Your **spirit body** holds a select memory of emotions carried over from previous lifetimes with the purpose of resolving past conflicts and releasing them. It also brings forth all the wisdom and knowledge from the previous lives but your spirit may not remember them at first. Remembrance comes with advanced soul development.

Your spirit duplicate remains with you throughout life. It rises up each night as you sleep to explore the world around you and returns just before you wake with dreams for you to record as your nightly excursions. This is partly the reason that every living creature must sleep. It is necessary for your spirit's energy to recharge. You actually have batteries like your cell phone that need recharging each night while your spirit takes a walk in the spirit world closest to earth. Many people have learned to Astral Travel where they can consciously take their spirit out of their body while it sleeps and travel wherever they desire.

I wish I could experience astral travel. I even took a weekend class in "Out-of-Body Travel." My friend claimed that I had done it. She said she talked to my spirit. But that couldn't be as I had no memory of the encounter. When I asked the instructor about it, he was puzzled also. I told him that I could go into a light trance state and do what some call "remove viewing." It is like I take my consciousness and travel. The instructor said it was called "mind travel" and was a fine way to gain information and for me to continue doing it.
So Raphael, can you speak a moment on this?

Indeed, Rae. You are very adept at leaving your body through your mind and travelling long distances even into the other dimensions. This is more than "mind travel." It is a greater form of gathering information from other realities or dimensions.

Some people worry that if they leave their body to travel they won't be able to return and might die.

Your spirit is connected to your physical body with a silver cord that is like the Yo-Yo's string snapping back into its case whenever the physical body is ready to awaken.

If you have had an out-of-body experience where you are consciously aware you are within your spirit as it lifts out of your physical body, you may at first experience fear. Do not be afraid. Many have experienced this phenomenon and have learned to enjoy travelling in the spirit body.

When your physical body no longer serves your soul's story, your spirit duplicate departs from the physical body by rising up and going to that heavenly dimension that has been prepared for you. You call this death. We call this merely a transition from sentient life into your true form of spirit. We will devote an entire chapter to the death experience at the end of this book.

As in all choices made by the soul via its physical expression—you—there are consequences that expand your conscience or, if you will, your list of what is right and good and what is not. The soul does not dictate things as good or evil. You do according to the beliefs you garnered from the influence of religious, parental, and educational teachings. Each experience gains your soul new knowledge that it stores, and in turn helps it grow from an infant with little to no knowledge of the physical realm, to an adult soul with many lifetimes that have gained it great wisdom. Again, this wisdom only comes from many lifetimes of experience within the physical dimension.

Getting back to the main topic: how do we maintain health in our physical body?

The body maintenance comes with daily responses to intake of food as well as your emotional energy at any given moment.

To help you appreciate your body, we have included ideas to ponder as well as suggestions for daily maintenance of your physical, mental, emotional, and spiritual bodies.

1. What you think, feel, believe, or expect to happen will become who you are spiritually, mentally, emotionally and physically. You are an energy being. Each thought creates energy that redefines who you are.

2. There are three types of fuel your body needs: 1) food with life-giving energy to feed the body; 2) sleep to refuel your spirit; and 3) emotional fuel to keep you happy, which is the greatest of all fuels.

3. When you bless your food, you alter the energy of it for the good of your body's smooth merging with its chemical elements.

4. Every thought has a corresponding electrochemical reaction in the brain which you feel in your body. You are an electrical machine as well as a chemistry laboratory. Divine energy is freely given and freely molded into whatever you perceive as truth.

5. Physical action begins with a thought that stimulates an emotion which results in a shift in an attitude toward life, which in turn molds your physical, mental, emotional and spiritual bodies…like an inside-out process.

6. By reconnecting with your soul, you can begin re-establishing communication with all the systems within the body. While it starts in the brain, there are many pathways that flow throughout the body carrying messages to maintain ultimate functioning of the body engine. By imaging this process as functioning perfectly, you can enhance it for greater health. We will speak more of this in the chapter on meditation.

7. Your brain at any one moment is performing around 400 billion actions without any conscious thought by you. This alone is reason to give praise to your marvelous Creator! We say unto you, fear nothing for the hand of God touches you and never lets it go.

What about pain within the body?

Pain serves the spirit in a multitude of ways. No one escapes pain while in a sentient body.

Pain offers great benefits through humble endurance by serving the soul with knowledge that can increase compassion for others.

When pain is severe, it forces the person to seek relief, which leads to more experiences with those in the medical community as well as those in the spiritual healing professions.

What is not known and is rarely revealed is how accidents and pain often serve to alter the path of the sentient being when the soul realizes it is not following the divine plan set forth for its advancement.

When my husband wanted me to quit teaching eight years earlier to be with him when he retired, I refused saying that I loved teaching. Although at the time it required me to live in my townhouse an hour away. Neither of us enjoyed the separation. But I was stubborn.

While I was living in my townhouse, we decided to renovate my husband's small ranch. On the first day in October, we were laying tar paper on the new addition. I straddled a six-foot ladder upon a scaffolding and used a staple gun to adhere the tar paper. The ladder tipped and I fell, breaking the 12th thoracic vertebrae.

It kept me from teaching for a few months. When I returned, my students were unruly from lack of discipline from many substitute teachers. It took me a month to let them know I was the boss and for things to return to my idea of classroom order.

At the end of that school year, I retired.

Thus, we were able to have Rae devote her complete attention to our work. We arranged for this accident. Now that may seem cruel for us to use such a pain-filled accident to change the direction of a life. And yet, we say unto you: **there are no accidents**. Each soul is divinely guided to gain as much knowledge as possible from the life. Sometimes when the human heads in the wrong direction, we will create a different scenario to bring the soul's plan back into focus. But not all accidents are because of the person going in the wrong direction. It can be to speed the soul along the path to enlightenment. As we have said earlier, near-death experiences have a profound effect on the soul's sentient self.

At this moment, I am experiencing another back injury. I foolishly neglected to recognize my limitations and lifted a heavy box of books in preparation for a book signing. It herniated a disk.

Yes. Poor choices can lead to physical injury. As always, we have used this accident for Rae to focus the time on completing this book.

This may seem to be "cruel and unusual punishment" when the person did nothing wrong. It is not. Rae has given her life to our work. When we need her undivided attention, we sometimes step in to create a situation that will give us just that.

You may wonder if that idea is working when you see the state of your world. Yet, perceive all the players and how they are making choices daily that either move them forward on their soul's journey or block them from achieving the goals they have set forth.

There are always consequences for your choices. This is indeed the whole process of incarnating—learning from your choices. You will always reap what you sow. When the conscience mind and your spirit have been constantly compromised, it can no longer discern right from wrong.

The human body suffers pain in many forms. When a limb is severed, the person can feel it itch for the spirit body still holds the energy of the limb and will reattach it when the physical life is over. Even as you sleep, your spirit limbs attach and you dream of being whole and healthy again.

We still see people trying to judge pain or disabilities as righteous results of wrongdoing. They hold fast to the concept of Karma because they believe in a God who sits upon a throne and declares who will enter heaven and who will be sent to hell.

Know this: God does not judge. We implore you: Do not judge others or your dear self. Like the frog in the kettle—when the heat is turned up, it does not know it is being cooked to death. Some may awaken only after they leave your Earth through death. And no...they will not experience a so-called Hell. They will experience love and compassion and patience while they review their life and become aware of when they started cooking in the waters of fear and anxiety and greed.

God is pure love. It cannot create anything other than love. Only you as a sentient being can create through the polarities of your planet and express all the emotions ranging from love to despair. These emotions do not exist in the other realms. Neither does pain.

Chapter 5
What About My Brain?

Why am I not as smart as I'd like to be? Although I did manage to get a couple of college degrees, I still feel quite stupid when it comes to math. Without a calculator, I'm lost.

Each mind has been created perfectly to serve the soul's story for it reflects the seeking of your greatest good this time around. Your brain is a receiver of divine inspiration much like the receiver of sound waves on your radio or phone. Your mind can pick up on another's thoughts and surprise you when the person suddenly calls and says he/she was thinking of you.

The mind has great power beyond your physical understanding of the brain and its functions in keeping the body's organs working.

Your Intellectual Aura

While in a consultation, we often show Rae the client's intellectual aura as a globe of amber light around the head. Artists of old presented this halo as those of saints and holy ones. All people have this halo but not all are saints!

Some auras have little flecks of brown floating within the aura in the shape of tiny squares, rectangles and triangles. This denotes self-doubt and self-deprecation which are caused by a lack of trust in self and in God.

Intellect versus Knowledge

To begin, let us clarify intellect versus knowledge. Scholars often equate knowledge and intelligence by the number of years spent in school earning degrees. There are many who have gained great knowledge without any degree or advanced education. We speak of the many craftsmen who study a trade and master it. We speak of skills gained from life experiences that increase the soul's knowledge of sentient life. All are valuable and everyone advances within their apprenticeship under the Master Creator. Retaining facts does not advance knowledge. Only experiences gained from emotional responses can add to your soul's growth.

The soul may choose a mind and intellect with less intelligence that will benefit their advancement toward becoming one with God. By the soul taking on the simplistic joys of a childlike mind it may be balancing a previous life where it had been overloaded with too much mental responsibility.

The Hemispheres of Your Brain

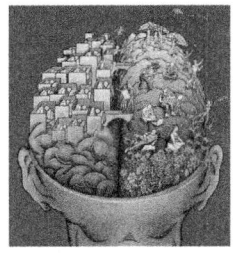

God has designed your magnificent computer-like brain specifically for your vehicle of expression in this lifetime. Your mind automatically regulates every organ in your body for the highest sustainable health.

The brain sends out energy waves to communicate with non-physical worlds allowing you to send messages telepathically to people hundreds of miles away.

We will not get too technical about the names and scientific function of the brain. We will speak only as to how you can make better use of it for your highest good.

The right and left hemispheres of the brain bring to the spirit and soul two different perceptions of your world. Too often, teaching methods have been directed to students who are left-brain dominant when they teach through lecture-style classes and written words. Those who are right-brain dominant need pictures, graphs and visual aids. If they do not have these learning tools, they may fall behind.

The Left Hemisphere: Mathematical, Logical, and Rational Thinking

Most engineers, mathematicians, scientists, or other detail-oriented people are left-brain dominant. The left hemisphere enables you to filter facts through the logical, factual sequencing of ideas. It is here that information is placed in literal interpretations with language-related ideas. This side of the brain gives structure and order to thoughts by labeling and classifying them. It deals with math and number relationships and calculations. It provides you with the critical analysis of new ideas. The left hemisphere of the brain enables you to make practical use of whatever you have learned or are learning. It allows you to make sense of information and place it within existing patterns.

The left hemisphere of the brain controls the right side of the body.

The Right Hemisphere: Intuitive, Creative, Artistic and Image Perceptions

Right brain dominant people tend toward artistic endeavors. They can be artists, architects, builders, writers, teachers, and speakers such as politicians or religious leaders.

The right hemisphere of the brain sends visual patterns and images to your mind. It holds the spatial information you need to see the world around you and is often the area where spontaneous, random, and open-ended ideas originate.

This is also your intuitive side which allows you to deal with the paradoxes and ambiguities you face in life.

The right hemisphere of the brain can tap into and process the universal consciousness allowing you to get the bigger picture of your world. If you allow it, the function of the right brain can help you see beyond your narrow frame of reference and experience a cosmic consciousness, or God Consciousness.

People who are right-brain dominant accept messages from both outer and inner senses. Ideas come to them in pictures, feelings, and symbols.

Once you understand how the right hemisphere sends ideas and visual pictures, you can begin to develop your intuition. Know that by using your right brain to bring in abstract information, your left brain can then translate that information into physical reality. The right hemisphere gives you extra-sensory perception (ESP), which sees beyond the reality in front of you. You may begin to have ideas about people which you did not know previously. You may begin to intuit what they might say or do.

Do not allow fear to enter your thought processes. Rejoice that you are using your entire brain as God intended it to be used—fully and fearlessly.

Balanced Hemispheres Unlock Your Soul's Treasure Chest of Creative Ideas

If you have a job that requires attention to detail, you will utilize your left brain. You need to balance it with creative endeavors like art or music or dance. Listening to music is often a way to engage your right brain. But if it only becomes background noise while you worry about your job or a loved one, you have shifted back to the left hemisphere of analyzing and criticizing, labeling and judging. These thoughts drain your energy.

Once you become aware of any negative thoughts, shift to the right hemisphere of your brain with an image of a beautiful place in nature such as gardens of your favorite flowers or a serene place near water in its natural environment. Breathe deeply, relax the body and soon you will become energized. This is the value of your right hemisphere's ability to imagine. This is how you bring abstract ideas into physical reality.

Exercise both hemispheres of your brain daily. Work with mathematical figures and then switch to reading a novel where you picture the characters acting out the story.

God designed you perfectly to be Its presence in your world. God lives within you, urging you daily to love freely, laugh joyously and choose wisely only that which advances your soul. Know which ideas bring you smiles. Know they are sent by God in Its desire for you to be happy.

Remember we have said that your purpose for being is to be happy! This requires using both hemispheres simultaneously and in balance.

Develop PMA

I've always said that I choose to have PMA instead of PMS!

It is always better to keep a **Positive Mental Attitude** about your body, your mind, and your beingness as a reflection of the Creator. Remember that you always have Free Will to choose what to think, do, or say at any given time. Learn to choose the inspirations from God that come to you through the right hemisphere of your brain. They usually come as an abstract idea in the form of a thought or pictures or a feeling or even a knowing.

Next, we will help you see how another side of your brain works as it rests at night while you sleep. It will help you understand what happens to your mind during each of the brain's transitions from a wake state into the different levels of the sleep state from dreams to a nearly comatose state almost like death and then back to dreams and back to a semi-wake state.

Sleep studies have found your brain moves through a 90-minute cycle in which you slip from one brain wave level to another, bringing dreams and deep, healing sleep. This explains why sleep is so essential to good health. It has been proven that a person can go insane without at least three house of sleep per night.

Beta Brain Waves

During your awake state, the conscious mind is very active observing the world around you, making choices, thinking about past, present and future scenarios. Your busy brain works at 15 to 21 Hz per second.

All your senses of sight, sound, smell, taste and touch are working with time-space awareness giving you impressions without conscious thought. Your mind sorts facts from opinions as you instantly analyze and label everything by deciding if it is truth or fiction or if it is good or bad or neutral. In this waking state, you make hundreds of decisions a day.

When the Beta mind refuses to be still, insomnia can result. Your mind continues to sort through the day's events, perhaps worrying about what happened that day or what might happen in the coming days. We will offer a solution to insomnia in the guided meditations later in this book. By focusing the Beta mind to concentrate on the mundane, the brain falls into boredom and eventually your body relaxes as your mind shuts down and you drift into the first level of sleep.

Alpha Brain Waves

In this first sleep state, your conscious awareness slips into a semi-conscious real of dreams that researchers call Rapid Eye Movement or REM sleep. Your brainwave cycle slows to fourteen and down to seven HZ per minute.

At this level of mind, if you remain awake, you can experience psychic awareness when your inner senses awaken. You can experience visions or daydreams where ideas flow and solutions are given. As you allow your mind to drift deeper, your spirit body lifts from your physical body and goes exploring bringing back dreams and ideas. Some people can remember their spirit's nightly journeys in this state of no-time or space awareness.

As you relax and allow your mind to drift into this first phase of sleep, the brain stops labeling anything as good or bad. It doesn't even have an opinion. It simply observes. The mind is busy with dreams as if you were watching a movie.

While the Beta or conscious mind observes the world around you through your five outer senses of sight, sound, touch, taste and smell, the Alpha dream-state awakens your five inner senses.

By consciously going to the Alpha state, you can reach a light form of mediation to access information from your angels and guides.

Our guided meditations utilize the alpha state of mind where you can awaken your imagination to bring you images and symbols. We will suggest how to keep the eyes open allowing you to be simultaneously in both the beta mind and the alpha mind. This method of meditation where you write down all you sense will help you decipher the images and symbolism to gain new knowledge and wisdom for your soul.

The challenge in this form of meditation is to stay awake while at the alpha brain level of dreaming. Your challenge is to keep your mind from slipping out of that semi-sleep state into the beta mind where you may try to analyze or decipher the meaning of the images that your right brain supplies.

In order to do creative work such as painting (either on walls or canvas) or writing or problem solving, the Alpha state of mind is where you need to go to find amazing answers. In this form of meditation, you will learn how to use both hemispheres for gaining greater knowledge and wisdom.

Theta Brainwaves

During sleep, the brain falls into an unconscious state where the mind has no time-space awareness and the brain waves slow from seven to four HZ cycles per second. This totally releases the conscious mind's need to comment and puts you into a deep trance state where channeling or astral travel is possible.

When a person can go into this state consciously and at will, they are said to be in a deep trance and can create amazing works of art or bring forth genius ideas. It is where people experience out-of-body travel where your spirit vacates your physical body and consciously takes your spirit body to travel outside your body called Out-of-Body Travel or OBE's.

Delta Brainwaves

The brain slows to an unconscious state with the brain cycles at only four to zero cycles per second. You have no sense perception while your body enters an automatic healing state. It is where God touches you to help the mind and body replenish and rejuvenate. Without this stage of sleep, the body and mind can become ill.

Why do people get dementia?

Dear ones, every illness or dysfunction of the physical body is caused by more than one thing and serves more than one purpose, most of which are not known to the human mind. Sometimes, your Council helped your soul plan dementia from before you were born. Sometimes it is the soul's way to escape an unbearable outcome it sees coming.

Most of the time, it is the result of the person's choices throughout the life. For example, it is well known now that cigarette smoking can cause lung cancer. Many souls did not know this at first and even after they learned of the consequences, they were so severely addicted it was almost impossible to stop.

Smoking can also cause heart attacks and other yet unknown illnesses.

We have spoken of this many times but medical science has not as yet accepted the fact that your emotions are the basis of your health with the exception of any pre planned ailments set up by your Council before you were born.

Illness serves the soul and is often triggered by unfulfilled emotional needs.

Your mind, soul and spirit are all contributing to your body's health and well-being. You are not always in control.

What happens to the brain when people go into a coma?

Again, there are often many reasons for a person experiencing a coma. Usually it is caused by some kind of brain trauma. Induced comas allow the swelling of the brain to recede so healing can take place.

Sometimes the soul chooses an accident for its sentient partner that can lead to a coma. It wants to explore other dimensions from its spirit duplicate's point of view. To do this, it has to leave the body but it does not want to sever the connection with it. They plan to come back with advanced knowledge or new spiritual gifts from the study of esoteric information elsewhere.

Another reason that a soul may decide to experience a brain injury is for the sake of scientific study. Before life began, the soul may set this up at a certain stage of the physical body's life.

Because the soul is not emotionally involved within the human life, it can seem to be insensitive to suffering and pain. It is. It can plan for its leading character to suffer and die as part of its story, just as authors of novels can even have their leading character die in the end.

What are these dimensions you speak of?

We refer to the different planes of your physical world and the dimensions within the spirit worlds.

You live in a dimension of time/space within the confines of your planet's gravitational pull.

Consider the many galaxies beyond your planet Earth. Each one is considered a vibrating dimension with unique characteristics that define its purpose and intent within the mind of God.

First, let us clarify our term dimension. We refer to physical dimensions as vibrational frequencies that hold physical matter within a physical world. Each planet within any galaxy is vibrating with a frequency that has its unique particles of matter that create a physical manifestation visible to human observation. Yet within that physical dimension, there are many planes of more subtle energies existing simultaneously with the unique make-up of the star or planet or asteroid or any other gathering of physical material.

The spirit dimension is of a rarer, faster-vibrating frequency of subtle matter that is invisible to physical eyes or telescopes. Within this dimension, there are many planes of existence according to its vibrational frequencies.

Mystics speak of this dimension as heaven. While it is merely a level of energy that the spirit explores on its way back to the soul dimension, it is again a faster vibration not only making it invisible to the physical eye, but beyond awareness of any human spirit until the spirit merges with the soul when it is ready to return to the soul's home. It cannot just visit at will. It would not be compatible with the vibratory energy of that powerful realm or dimension.

Many speak of dimensions beyond your physical world as if they were stepping-stones to enlightenment or soul development. They talk about the "Age of Aquarius" or the "Fifth Dimension." They all exist simultaneously because souls are in different stages of development in their exploration of physical worlds.

People such as Robert Monroe have written about their adventures to other non-physical dimensions. It led him to teach others how to leave the body and allow the mind-consciousness to explore the dimensions he had carefully marked according to his definition of the dimensional experience.

As we've said before, Edgar Cayce induced a coma-like trance state when he allowed his body to fall into a deep sleep and have his spirit vacate to allow another spirit to enter and use his vocal cords to bring through healing remedies for others. His guides channeled knowledge about other dimensions, revealing new information about dreams, and about previous lifetimes that were affecting a person's health in the present life.

Do previous lifetimes have an effect upon illness in the present lifetime?

Yes, but only if it serves your soul in bringing you greater knowledge and wisdom.

Life within the physical is all about learning to work within the denser dimensions. We angels along with others in spirit help in any way we can.

For example, Rae channels our abstract thoughts by transcribing them into words. Although we use her vocabulary and speak to her in words, we often send images instead. You have experienced the flash of an idea that took several words to explain what you saw or sensed or simply knew.

Having now studied how amazingly God has created your human brain, perhaps you can begin to think of thoughts as patterns of energy brought together to create an image or an abstract idea as a method of gathering information, solving problems and bringing forth amazing creations.

We predicted that in the coming times, you would find more transparency of thoughts and actions with your reporting of news. We saw it as heralding the rising of consciousness. It means a new awakening of humankind to their real identity as sentient beings who are all fixed within God's divine mind.

This Time of Times will inspire and uplift a multitude of spirits across the globe to follow their soul's inner seeking of honesty, integrity and truth.

We encourage you to do likewise. Listen to your thoughts. Choose to entertain only the ones that inspire you to be happy and to do good deeds.

We also encourage you to record your dreams. Your angels and guides help you resolve emotional frustration through those nightly visions. We will speak more fully on dreams in a later chapter and will provide an interpretation of the symbols used to help you interpret your nightly visions. You can then utilize this gift of knowledge to lead your soul into divine wisdom.

Since we have said how negative emotions can deplete your energy, our next chapter will focus on these powerful bodies of emotional energy that can raise or lower your level of consciousness. By becoming consciously aware of your emotional state at any given moment, you have more control over your life and the impact of your actions.

Chapter 6
What is Spirit Consciousness?

Definition of Consciousness

Spirit consciousness is an awareness of your spirit within that carries all your emotions.

Consciousness *can be technically defined as a state of awareness of the world around you through the use of your five senses to gather information, sort it into categories, label it, judge it as good, bad or indifferent according to your beliefs and experiences, and then to act upon your conclusions.*

"Raising Consciousness" *can be defined as altering your state of awareness to a super-conscious state of mind where you use your additional inner senses to become aware of that which the physical world cannot define.*

"Higher Consciousness" *may be defined as an altered state of awareness of God bringing you inner peace, love and joy.*

Advantages of a "Raised" Consciousness

Many good things start to happen when you raise your consciousness and begin to use your inner senses.

- *Your understanding of life around you will widen so you can begin to see the bigger picture.*

- *Your intuition sharpens as you become aware of your soul sending new ideas for solving everyday problems.*

- *Your soul sends inner visions or "pictures" where your welfare is concerned.*

- *You develop a sense of knowing how to live a happier, more joy-filled life.*

- *Your soul will increase your inner sensing, which will bring you a keen awareness of the subtle energies around you and others.*

- *Your soul will remind you how to stay balanced during stressful times.*

- *Your soul will bring to you an awareness of itself and its plan for your life.*

- *You will awaken to a driving need to an increased sense of well-being through beautifying your mind and your surroundings.*

- *You will experience a great thirst for knowledge and be led to find answers to long-held questions that will nag at you until you're satisfied.*

- *A higher sense of integrity will grow within you. It will not allow you to be dishonest with anyone in any way, especially with yourself.*

- *A higher sense of compassion and tolerance will allow you to understand another's position, thus making detachment easier and confrontations less frequent.*

- *An increased confidence in decision-making will lead to better choices with results that are more of your liking.*

- *Your creative ideas will "pop!" with the willpower to follow them through to physical reality.*

- *Your relationships will either strengthen or dissolve.*

- *Your energy will increase, giving you time to do more things of your choosing.*

The Story of the 100th Monkey

Scientists have long been searching for where we have our consciousness. One such study began back in 1952 when Japanese scientists worked with monkeys on two separate islands that they had named A and B. These islands were far apart and movement between them was not possible for the monkeys.

They began by rowing bushels of sweet potatoes out to the islands and dumping them on the beach. Then they rowed back a way and observed what the monkeys would do. The little animals were shy at first, but eventually their curiosity got the better of them and they happily nibbled on the potatoes and then carried them back into the jungle.

The next time the scientists arrived, the monkey waited until the men had left in their boats before they dashed out to retrieve the potatoes and scatter back into the dense jungle.

Then one day, a little monkey on island A washed the sand off the sweet potato before eating it.

On their next visit, a few more washed the sand from their potatoes before eating them. This excited the scientists.

And then one day, all the monkeys on island A washed their food before eating it. At that precise moment, all the monkeys on island B began washing their sweet potatoes.

This began the concept of quantum physics in that a concept or thought arrived at by a large number of people could be suddenly transferred to others.

The scientists were baffled but declared that here was a leap in consciousness that they labeled, "The Hundredth Monkey."

This experiment gives you a clue as to how the divine Mind works. When enough people have raised their consciousness, this phenomenon will suddenly spread throughout your world.

We say unto you dear one, the scientific community is now beginning to understand this concept. Much is being said about "Mindfulness," which is another word for this 100th Monkey consciousness. And yet the scientific community still does not believe it has found the true meaning of consciousness for it requires the visible essence of your spirit and soul. Until the scientific world can understand we are all made of God's pure Spirit that dwells within us, they will never understand who and what we are—you as a sentient being with a soul and we as angels.

We have said how your spirit is an exact duplicate of your physical body. Your spirit also holds your soul's awareness of God while perceiving it through a prism of all your emotional experiences within the physical body and into the afterlife.

Like the picture shown at the beginning of this chapter, each night when you sleep, your spirit lifts out of your body and is free to explore both the physical and non-physical worlds.

While your body is in the deepest vibrations of sleep, your spirit travels into unseen dimensions. During this deep sleep, God charges up your energy centers which are like the batteries charging up your cell phone. These batteries line up along the spine of both your physical and spirit bodies as shown in the diagram below.

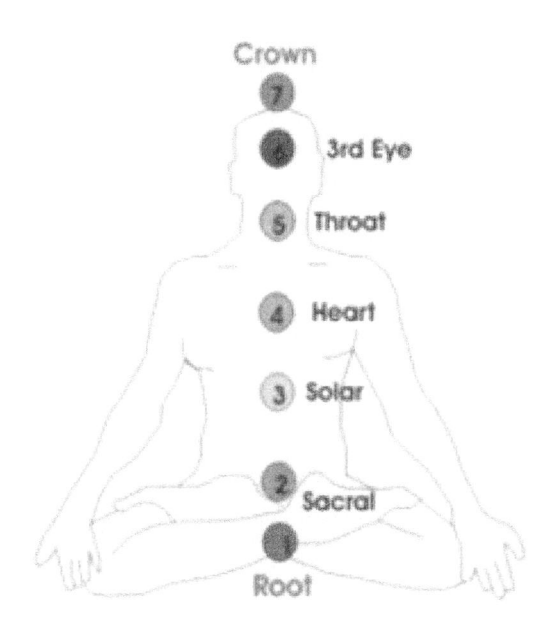

Crown
7
6 3rd Eye
5 Throat
4 Heart
3 Solar
2 Sacral
Root

Your batteries are moving orbs of divine light. They are called Chakras (pronounced Chuck-rus), which is a Sanskrit word meaning wheels of light. You may compare them to the circuit breakers in your home. The divine energy surges through your body's electrical wiring called *meridians* that connect the Chakra to its assigned organs of your body, keeping it balanced and healthy.

It is only when you experience continued stressful emotions such as anger, worry, or fear that you can cause a blockage of the vital flow of divine energy throughout your body. This will result in physical imbalance and eventually disease.

While souls have a vibrational frequency far above any measurement of these batteries, your Chakras resonate to your musical scale. As we have said previously, spiritual healers are now using sound to heal the human body's energy and bring it back to health.

Cleanse Your Batteries Nightly

We strongly encourage each of you to cleanse these seven Chakras each night by simply visualizing them as sparkling jewels in all the colors of the rainbow. Define the anxieties of your day that may have clouded the brilliance of your inner jewels of light. Then imagine you take a magic cloth and polish each jewel to remove the grit of negativity from that energy center.

Your Gift of Second Sight

Each of you have intuitive powers. People speak of them as your **inner senses**. **Clairvoyance** is from the French term meaning clear seeing. **Clairaudience** means clear hearing. **Clairsentience** relates to clear sensing and **Claircognizance** refers to clear knowing. People reveal these senses when they say, "I saw that coming," or "I feel," or "I sense" or "I knew it!"

Your spirit holds the gift of second sight. It is aware of the faster vibrating energies of these inner senses and holds awareness of the presence of spirits of those who have left their physical bodies. Some spirits hovering nearby may not be deceased but only sleeping and it is their spirit that may meet with yours during the deep sleep state. You may remember this encounter as a dream. It may seem quite real—because it is.

Those of you who are aware of all or some of these gifts might be called to use them to help others. You may be labeled as a psychic or a medium or a channel.

We caution you: never offer your wisdom unless you are called upon to do so by God and are first given permission by the person. Otherwise, you would be interfering in the life story of another and this is not good work. **If you are asked to intuit or give your insight for a person,** do so after first offering a silent prayer asking God to bring you truth and wisdom. Then, quietly go within and allow ideas and images to float into your consciousness. Only then may you have complete confidence to share what you receive.

Everything is vibrating energy. You may feel spirit as a chill you call gooseflesh. It may not be from the cold but from the presence of a disembodied spirit trying to contact you. Do not be afraid. Speak with love and ask how you may help them. Then, quietly listen as ideas present themselves in your mind sometimes through visions. Be cautious to decipher the difference between positive thoughts that uplift and inspire and negative thoughts that drain your energy and leave you feeling uncomfortable.

While your physical planet is vibrating at the slowest energy level, your body's energy flows faster, and your spirit vibration is faster still with your soul's energy vibrating even faster. Each vibration has its own plane of existence that we call dimensions. For example, your soul dwells in the fastest vibration of all those other energies, while your spirit belongs to the vibrational level we call the Astral plane, and your physical body dwells within the slowest energy vibration of the Earth in order for you to live on your planet with gravity keeping you from floating away.

Where do visions come from?

Visions come from the mind of God through your guardian angel in the form of ideas or visuals. They often just pop into your mind. As an example of some abstract idea you are trying to convey to another, it may sometimes come in the form of a clip from a movie. You may use the words, "It's like when…" and then you describe the scene.

For example, we once sent Rae a picture of the musical duo called Sonny and Cher. Rae puzzled over the image until we suggested she have a sunnier disposition and not be afraid to share our wisdom with others.

When a vision comes to you that has not yet been manifested, it may be for you to consider bringing into your world. Artists find this process quite common as do architects, designers, and other creative people.

Many call Rae a visionary not only because of her ability to see other's lives, but because of all the different forms of artwork she has brought into her world. Visions are most often used in her daily work with us as we seek to help those who ask our wisdom concerning their lives. It is why she has insisted we use pictures scattered throughout this book. She knows how many people learn faster through visuals rather than words.

For example, to help a new client believe that what Rae sees is real, we often describe something in their home or their car that will give them confidence that we are truly working with them. This form of confirmation is most often visual.

An Example

In 1992, after Rae prayed to find a spiritual rug for her meditation room, we sent her a vision. She quickly drew the design of a rug on a piece of paper. Although she had never seen this kind of rug-making before, we followed with visions of how to make the rug by pulling narrow strips of 100% recycled wool through a backing of burlap.

Our next inspiration sent her to the nearest craft store where she fully expected to find the materials and begin her new project. Although we knew that no one she would meet had ever heard of her vision's form of hooking, the meeting with each person was part of God's divine plan to bring her light to others.

A word on this. Each interaction with a stranger, each genuine smile and even a nod that says, "I see you," can lift a person's spirits to instantly smile and nod back.

Each encounter you have with another is an exchange of divine energy.

With Rae's smile and genuine interest in others, those encounters became a blessing. The salesclerks kept shaking their heads, saying they only knew of rugs made by use of a latch-hook using wool yarn to create a shaggy-type rug. But the clerks were left with a smile and a comment on what a nice person that lady was. Their energy was raised by her presence.

You are constantly exchanging energy with others. A smile will increase energy. A frown will decrease it.

Rae believed in her vision from us. She did not give up. She and her husband visited several craft stores even going from their home in Michigan across the bridge to Canada. Alas, no one there had ever heard of rug hooking made from strips of wool cloth.

We tested her determination as she continued to search and only found blank faces. Yet, she pursued our vision and we rewarded her with an idea to search for it in the library. (Google was not known until 1998).

She found a teacher who owned a store an hour from her home. The display of colorful, already-cut, light-weight wool filled Rae with joy. She had four lessons before she was on her own to complete her four-foot by six-foot rug.

We were not done yet. The finding of the wool was not the only reason we sent Rae with our vision. In exchange for her lessons, we gave the woman and her daughter several hours of our messages that uplifted and inspired them.

We showed Rae a vision of a silk rug. She had never even heard of rugs made of silk and when she asked the teacher about it, the woman said she owned a silk rug. This again gave the woman confidence in Rae's clairvoyant abilities.

No encounter with a stranger just happens. We set it up if even for a few moments as an opportunity to exchange loving energy. This was so with all the salesclerks Rae encountered. We always passed blessings in divine energy. We offer you an opportunity to reach out with compassion and joy to all you meet.

Thus, for Rae, these encounters brought many people to Rae to learn of our messages. She also enjoyed learning an almost-lost art form. It began an entire career of teaching others to become hookers. Her husband loved telling his co-workers that he had married a hooker!

In 1994, we inspired Rae to submit her Symbols' Rug to the Rug Hooking Magazine's yearly selection of rugs for their book called *A Celebration of Hand-Hooked Rugs*. Individually each of the judges voted for her rug to become a part of the book. They said later that they had never seen anyone tackle so large a rug for their first one nor to have it so artistically balanced.

Now dear reader, perhaps you can understand how following an inspiration, although it may seem impossible, can lead to amazing experiences you would never have believed possible.

We say unto you: follow your heart's desires. God placed them there for you to practice becoming Its co-creator within physical worlds. New ideas may stretch your beliefs and test your endurance and patience, but the rewards can be far beyond your expectations.

Rae's rug becomes an excellent example of persistence in following through with an idea no matter what obstacles may try to stop you.

Remember, dear soul, your purpose for being here is to become God's co-creator of goodness and beauty.

When you ask what your purpose is for being here in this world, you expect a single answer in some form of accomplishment you have come to do. Not so. You are here to explore many ideas; to experience many encounters with others; and to bring love, peace and harmony into your personal world.

Being a "hooker" was not Rae's purpose for coming to the planet. She came for thousands of reasons just like you. Every time you create something that brings you joy it is an example of your purpose for being here—to bring beauty and goodness into your everyday world. Rae's rug was just one example of how she persisted in following her intuition and her visions in creating something beautiful. We say unto you: **Trust** is the key word here. **Trust** that when you are inspired to try something new, you will succeed. **Trust** you will be divinely led to reach that new goal. **Trust** there will be many blessings because of your persistence in following God's plan for your life.

Above is Betty Rae's four-foot by six-foot rug called *Symbols*. The original design was conceived in 1992 and completed in 1993. It is made of new and recycled wool cut into 3/32" strips and hooked through burlap.

Divine inspiration is constantly flowing to you with answers to your questions and concerns. The trick is to pay attention to your thoughts. Although you have billions of thoughts in and out of your brain on any given day, begin to become aware of them. Sort out those that are positive versus those that are negative. Which do you have more often? This will answer many questions as to why things happen as they do. Your thoughts are constantly creating your life. Those that you repeat often become a solid block of energy ready to manifest into a physical reality. When you hold a thought with great passion and enthusiasm, with joyous excitement or fierce hatred, with strong determination that it is a "fact" and you hold fast to it—it becomes reality for good or ill.

This is the wonderful reality of Rae's rug and becomes a visual example of this concept. She held forth our vision with joy and enthusiasm until the vision became a reality.

Chapter 7
Why Did Pandora Open That Darn Box?

Your emotions are your spirit's expression of your consciousness.

There is a fable about a beautiful box given to a girl called Pandora. Her instructions were to guard it and keep it tightly locked. Under no circumstances was she to open the box.

Of course, curiosity got the better of her. It is said that when she opened it, all the evils of humankind escaped, making it impossible for her to capture them and put them back.

What are considered "all the evils of humankind?"

Our negative human emotions! *Although we do not consider them evil, they can create havoc when they spill out of you without warning expressing anger; jealousy; hatred; bigotry, and so forth. You cannot call angry words or actions back. You cannot reason your envy or jealousy back into their box. You may suppress them and shove them down into your solar plexus until your stomach aches. Or you may pretend they do not exist until your body screams in pain.* **Unresolved negative emotions**

create anxiety which can lead to discomfort and eventually illness within the body.

The inventors of "Emotional Freedom Technique" knew that negative emotions blocked your meridians which prevented the flow of God's healing energy from connecting your energy centers into your meridians and vital organs. As we said earlier, your body's energy centers are like the circuit breakers in your home. Your electrical wiring is your body's meridians. Negative emotions are like those foods that cause cholesterol to block your arteries and thus can cause a heart attack or other damage to your body.

Negative emotions can do the same thing.

On the positive side, emotions give your spirit body amazing powers of expression. God designed the human experience to include this extra connection to Itself to act as the **consciousness** of your soul through **your spirit** that senses energy and declares if it is good or evil usually from the emotional responses from the act or event. These definitions may change as the soul gains more knowledge through awareness of your spirit's emotional reactions to life through the vibrating energy of your intellect. Each emotional experience advances the knowledge and wisdom of your soul throughout all its phases of human growth.

Your spirit duplicate is free to travel while your body sleeps. All humans and animals must sleep in order to recharge their energy for the next day's adventures.

When your negative emotions become like a runaway horse with the bit in its teeth, it takes the reins from the rider (your mind and spirit) and goes full speed ahead kicking up dust to muddy your precious jewels of vital energy. Your body and emotions grow malnourished and eventually starved from you withholding of God's nourishing love.

We encourage you to become aware of all negative thoughts and anxieties. Once recognized, you can begin to replace these debilitating emotions with positive thoughts called affirmations. These are statements of positive thoughts or actions to replace negative ones. You may argue that if you are angry, how can one replace it with a positive thought that is not a lie? If you hate something, how can you love it?

Change your mind set and open to new ideas.

This is where your gift of free will becomes activated. You choose how to think—not how to feel! Your emotions come unbidden. As we've said before, negative emotions can only be transformed into positive emotions through loving them. You can recognize your anger's source and by loving yourself in recognizing your need to express fear or a need may not be met or just because you cannot reason with someone or because someone refuses to follow your good advice...or...then you are being given the opportunity to let go of that person, step off their stage and go sit in the audience and joyously observe their life without your interference. If their actions create a problem in your life, you have other choices: you can demand their actions cease, or point out your discomfort and why you need them to stop their actions, or if you are trying to change them for your own comfort, you can give it up and walk away and let them be perfect exactly as they are.

Since you do not carry negative emotions into the next world, you must wait for your next expedition to your planet to release them. Before you entered the physical world, your soul selected certain unresolved emotional issues to explore. It packed them into your spirit body. Some emotions may involve the return of an advisory or even an enemy from a previous lifetime. In the proper moment within your soul's story, your angels will bring this adversary upon your Earth's stage and only then when your spirit must confront them will your advanced wisdom see them with a new perspective and thus heal the negative emotion.

You cannot put them back into their box. You can only love them back.

Beloved souls, we have already shared with you the existence of your **eternal spirit** and have spoken of how powerful your spirit's range of emotions can be. Emotions play such an important role in your life that we shall come back to them again and again.

Recall how we have said your spirit body holds a portion of your soul's energy replicating your physical body and yet vibrating too quickly for the human eye to see.

Know also that your spirit becomes the home of all your beliefs and every emotion you have or will experience within the total spectrum of energy from dark to light from despair to joy.

We repeat: Souls do not experience emotions. It is why the soul cannot fully understand the feelings expressed by its spirit. It can empathize but cannot experience the rollercoaster ride your spirit takes with its emotions. You cannot intellectually reason away your emotions.

This then becomes your challenge—not to put the emotions back into Pandora's box, but to **transmute them into love** through the embracing and acceptance of each new experience as a gift of knowledge. Know that each emotional experience begets wisdom that advances you along your journey into mastership.

Be at peace dear one. Your spirit duplicate will continue after death and will take with it a suitcase full of emotions.

Although in the afterlife where there are no polarities, the spirit will experience only positive emotions and thus create a heaven for you.

Indeed, emotions never sleep. Your spirit never sleeps. It lifts from your unconscious form each night to freely explore whatever your spirit desires. When it returns, it will bring back images and ideas in what you call dreams or nightmares. It views these out-of-body nightly excursions without your conscious mind's awareness and will perceive it through your emotions freely without judgment. This awakening of your soul's curiosity of the unknown helps it let go of negative emotions.

The Creator uniquely designed you to manifest your desires and ideas into your physical world through this connection with your spirit self.

In a wide range of emotions, below we define the energy associated with each one as the fuel that keeps your body and spirit active. Your brightest, highest frequency of Inner Peace reflects a full tank of energy, but the chart reveals how you proceed down the list into a decreasing emotional energy that leads into the slowest darkest energy of Despair where you will experience a completely empty tank of spiritual fuel.

Set your goal to become aware of the contents of your own personal Pandora's Box. Become aware of all negative emotions and choose to eliminate them from your daily life.

This means putting a guard on your thoughts. It means accepting and loving yourself as perfect right now. Know that your soul and spirit stretch and grow through each new awareness of God's amazing plan for your life.

As you bring your emotions into a higher state of consciousness, you will expand on the positive ones and slowly release the negative.

Think of your emotions as the engine that drives an idea into physical reality.

While fear can shut down an idea in a second, joy can fuel your emotions with great passion and excitement that can drive the idea into reality. We cannot speak too often of this truth. Therefore, we again spend time with you on a study of how your emotions can either serve you or become a barrier to having your needs met.

Below we have created a way of checking to see how your emotions are affecting your engine's fuel level. If you are registering the negative emotions, your engine is running on very little fuel. You may feel tired, fuzzy headed, lethargic, and even unable to get out of bed. Doctors call this depression. They may prescribe medicines to overcome your negative emotions. For some people, medical help is necessary. Those with a chemical imbalance within the brain need a chemical antidote to raise the consciousness out of those extreme mood swings in order to receive our inspirations and uplifting messages.

Only with a tank full of positive emotions can you bring forth the desires of your heart which are put there by God for you to create.

While certain emotions may be labeled as uncomfortable, negative and to be avoided, all emotions are gifts from God. They act as your GPS warning system when your spirit is low on energy, like the fuel in your automobile. To fill up your tank, we suggest you take time to meditate, to walk in nature, to laugh out loud, to get up and clean out a closet or a drawer. When you do anything constructive, you will snap out of the lower vibration and refuel your energy tank.

Emotions Equal Energy:
Check your emotional energy gauge.
Happy Emotions = a Full Tank

Peace: Inner peace holds the highest sense of euphoria for the soul.

Joy: May seem to be a fleeting come-and-gone experience, but once experienced strive to bring it forth more often.

Unconditional Love: is without judgment or strings attached. It holds no conditions or emotional need from another. It accepts the divine spirit within as perfect and complete within God.

Harmony: is an inner song revealing that all is flowing well in your life.

Humor: displays a sense of fun, of being able to laugh at your mistakes and slowly eliminating self-judgment and self-doubt.

Optimism: is knowing that all is well regardless of what others may think.

Trust: is a belief in another's integrity and honesty, of knowing they will not betray you or think ill of you if you do something wrong.

Appreciation: is a sense of gratefulness, of giving thanks and acknowledgement and appreciation for God's daily gifts.

Curiosity: is an inner urge to know more, to seek answers to inner questions about the world around you. After all, you are the explorer of all the wonders of your planet and your place in it.

Desire: is a wishing for, or a longing for, a person, place or thing, or hoping for a specific future outcome.

Passion: is an intense drive to fulfill a desire, an almost obsessive compulsion.

Your Emotional Energy Tank
Is half full if you are experiencing...

Skepticism: is not accepting an idea or theory until proven scientifically, factually or experientially.

Anxiety: is a fear that one's needs or those of another will not be met.

Being Overwhelmed: is feeling overburdened with too much to do and not enough time to do it.

Lust: is a passionate desire for experiencing physical pleasures without regard to the consequences.

Anger: is a fierce belief that a need will not be met, causing the person to lash out at another who is believed to be responsible.

Acceptance: is a letting go of trying to do it yourself and allowing divine help to intercede.

Discouragement: reflects a lethargic belief that this is "as good as it gets. Why try to change it?"

You are Almost on an Empty Tank
If you are experiencing...

Cynicism: is a belief that what can go wrong will go wrong.

Doubt: is a lack of trust in one's self, in others or in God.

Apathy: is the loss of any interest in creating new ideas or having new experiences.

Depression: is a lethargy that can immobilize and drain energy due to a belief that life is hopeless and will never get better.

Despair: is total belief that nothing matters, and all is lost.

For example, anger can drain your energy but when used to right a wrong, the euphoria at overcoming evil can refuel it. The basic reason for an expression of anger occurs because of unresolved frustration that a need has not been met. When one cannot verbalize a need, anger may result with building frustration. When the need still is not verbalized, it can become destructive.

Never allow another's anger or abuse or defamation to become acceptable actions. Physical and emotional offences often are resolved in dissolution of marriages or the birth new laws against marital violence and your system of justice is made clear in this matter.

Chapter 8
Why Do I Have Dreams?

While your Beta or conscious mind observes the world around you through your sense of sight, sound, touch, taste and smell, your Alpha state of mind observes those same things and spins out a range of positive and negative emotions as we have shown in the previous paragraph. Your dreams help you let go of fear and every-day cares to allow you to hear God's messages.

While in the wake state or Beta consciousness, you gather information and either react to it immediately or store it in the mind's data bank for later reference. The mind, as we have already observed, is one of the most wondrous mechanisms the Creator has manifested.

Now the Alpha mind is an entirely different story and one with which we need to become very familiar. At the Alpha level of mind, you begin to function at a state of heightened awareness where all your **inner senses are activated to add to the information arising from your outer senses.**

Since the Alpha mind is most often bringing you to the sleep state, the trick here is to use it as a tool for meditation by entering that state without falling asleep! We will go into a deeper understanding of meditation later with many examples given that will give you opportunities to practice lowering your brainwaves while lifting your mind and emotions out of the state of fear and doubt. The Alpha state is associated with paranormal consciousness, intuition, daydreams, visions, and, of course, dreams.

The sleep state at the Alpha level of mind is an essential function in maintaining health and well-being. Dreams are your other life that some claim is more real than your waking life. It is what scientists have called REM sleep, or Rapid Eye Movement, which they observed when a person was dreaming.

If you do not know how to interpret your dreams or even remember them, we will give you suggestions on how to do so in this chapter. You may be amazed at how closely your soul and your angels are working with you through dreams to bring about solutions to problems and answers to prayers.

Wise souls have suggested that you could also look at your waking life as though it were a dream, catching those symbolisms, or play on words, or coincidences and serendipitous moments as gifts from God. Symbolism is the name of the game here. We will help you become more aware of symbols we send throughout your life to awaken your inner senses.

Look at your world now as if you were in a waking dream in which everything you see or hear is a message from God and your angels.

Dreams Change Perspectives

Dreams are a way of helping you change your perspective. For over seven years, we encouraged Rae to study her dreams. She kept a dream journal in a three-ring binder where we encouraged her to record her dreams and taught her how to create a dream dictionary. For example, we revealed how a car in her dream referred to her waking personality. While a truck stood for her work personality. She filed this information under Vehicles. We revealed to her how we can use this new vocabulary of night visions to communicate with her soul. We suggest that you do likewise.

Dream research has shown that you have dreams twice every 90-minute segment.
"Dreams can be so real, it's scary," said one client after she revealed a dream of watching the space shuttle having to abort twice before it took off. She watched horrified as it went up and then came back down and crashed. It frightened her enough to call us about it. We said to envision the spacecraft taking off successfully. When she heard on the news how a space launch had to be aborted twice but was finally launched successfully, she was dumbfounded and grateful that she had done as we had suggested.

Whenever you receive a precognitive dream of disaster, spend time envisioning loving energy surrounding the situation, and thus change it if it is for the highest good of all concerned. You do not see life as God does. Death and tragedy do not have the same emotional responses of your soul that can see the bigger picture.

Many spiritual books relate the story of angels interceding within sentient beings' life experiences. An angel admonished Joseph not to be afraid to take Mary, his fiancée, as his wife although knowing she was pregnant, and he was not the father. Later, he received another dream when an angel told him to pack up his wife and child and move out of the country! Joseph paid attention to his dreams a third time when the angel gave him the all clear sign so that he could take his family home again.

Daniel of the Old Testament gained quite a reputation as a dream interpreter. Prince Thatmes also believed in dreams when he inscribed a dream on a stone tablet before the Great Sphinx of Gizeh in Egypt around 1450 BC. He wrote of a dream that he felt important enough for his people to know about centuries later.

Recorded throughout all the writings of ancient cultures and civilizations, you will find stories of dreams and dreamers. Greek mythology placed great emphasis upon dreams. Many called upon Aesclepius, the god of healing, to grant a dream that would tell the person how to heal the body.

How to Remember and Interpret Your Dreams

To show your angels and guides that you are serious about gaining new knowledge through your dreams, we suggest that you place a notebook beside your bed with a pen and a small glass of water. Just before you are ready for bed, drink **half** *of the water while you mentally say, "I intend to remember and understand my dream. Thank you, angels for helping me in this resolve."*

When you awaken, even if it is in the middle of the night, lie perfectly still, breathe deeply to allow the dream to return to your mind as you say, "I will recall my dreams vividly and with perfect understanding."

Then slowly take your pen and write down the basic vision of the dream <u>in present tense.</u> For example, instead of saying, "I <u>was walking</u> down a dark road and to my right <u>was</u>..." say, "I am walking down a dark gravel road. To my right I see..." Then, write out the scenario in as much detail as possible as if you were still in the dream seeing and experiencing it in the present time.

Script Your Dreams

Next, relax your body and bring back the dream as though you were entering another dimension and could sit down with each dream person, place, or thing and have a conversation with it. Ask why it appeared in your dream and what wisdom it can share with you. This is where you need a lot of trust along with a bit of imagination.

For example, even a chair may have a gift of wisdom for you by saying, "We encourage you to rest more often."

Often dreams are a means of expressing hidden emotions such as anger, frustration, or fear. In these other-worldly scenarios, your spirit can vent frustrations without causing damage to the people you love and care about. If you continuously have dreams of anger and frustration, perhaps you are being encouraged to make drastic changes in your life.

I experienced a nightmare where I found myself in a dark unfinished attic room with an open stairway to my right and on my left was a low slanted roof that caused me to bend over to avoid falling down the stairwell. Suddenly, a rat the size of a large cat appeared out of the darkness baring its teeth ready to attack me. I grabbed up a stick and thrust it at the rat to keep it away, but it was useless. The rat kept coming at me.

Finally, I thrust the stick in the rat's eye and stopped it. I ran down the stairs into what looked like a large, empty car-sales room with walls of glass all round. I yelled, "Get out! Get out!"

End of dream.

I almost didn't decipher the dream because of the terror it had caused me. But finally, I got up quietly so as not to disturb my husband, went into the bathroom with my notebook and scripted the dream like a scene in a movie:

Betty Rae: *Rat, why are you in my dream? You scared me.*

Rat: *I represent your fears and they <u>are</u> scaring you.*

Betty Rae: *But why did I push that stick into your eye?*

Rat: *The eye represents your perception of life. That is how you express fear. Change your viewpoint and you eliminate your fears.*

Betty Rae: *Okay… But why did I yell, "Get out! Get out!" when I got downstairs?*

Rat: *In the future, you will get out this dream many times to help people understand not only their dreams but their fears as well.*

And, indeed, Rae has brought forth this dream quite often when we encouraged her clients to record their dreams.

How to Interpret Your Dreams

Go back through your dream story and look for <u>words</u> that may have a double meaning such as the rat representing Rae's fears. Look for <u>objects</u> with a double meaning such as the eye may represent perception or perhaps what some call, the Third Eye representing intuition or inner seeing, rather than the physical eye.

Dreams are a powerful connection with your soul. Once you begin to pull them into your waking life and garner the gems of wisdom within them, you create a link with your soul that grows daily.

Over the years, we have helped Rae interpret people's dreams and taught them how to discover the wonderful wisdom within them. We are often disappointed when people do not pay attention to the wisdom we send through their dreams. It is like we have sent you a personal letter and you throw it in the wastebasket unopened.

The rat dream gave Rae a great wisdom at the time when fears were ruling her life. Her marriage was causing her all kinds of physical and emotional pain. This dream allowed her to begin paying closer attention to those adrenaline rushes so that she began to shift her awareness away from fear and into inner peace.

Become aware of how your negative emotions can be a gift of wisdom.

Below are several types of dreams that may help you interpret what your angels are sending you each night.

Emotional Dreams

An **emotional dream**, like Rae's rat dream, can reflect your frustrations or anger concerning someone or something. It can express your outrage about an injustice done to you. It can reflect your desire to get revenge knowing you are helpless to do so when awake. Emotions do not have a conscience. In your dreams, you can fight, mutilate, and even kill another. Violent dreams can sometimes reflect what you are doing to yourself.

Rae's friend shared her dream where she saw a stranger approaching with a bag over its head. It pointed a gun at her. She was fearful for her life.

When Rae discussed the symbolism, we suggested the friend bring back the dream as clearly as she could. When she was ready, Rae suggested she approach the stranger and take the bag off from its head.

The friend relaxed and let her imagination go back into the dream to do as we had suggested. Suddenly, the friend gasped and blurted, "It's me!" You could say she was *shooting herself in her foot*, a clique that you could be your own worst enemy.

We revealed to Rae that her friend's spirit was waiting for her to confront her fears of having breast cancer where she might die. She staunchly remained in strict denial of this truth. She did not want to leave her family and new grandchildren. Thus, the bag over her head represented her refusal to see the truth. Eventually she did die of breast cancer.

Most emotional dreams and dreams of violence are the result of unresolved conflicts or fears that a personal need may not be met.

Spiritual Dreams

A **spiritual dream** is one that gives you a message concerning your spirit self. We sent one to Rae with a vision of a lamb outside in the cold and snow in the front of her house. She went outside, took it by the scruff of the neck and gently led it inside the fence where it suddenly disappeared. We helped her interpret the lamb to symbolize the Lamb of God that she had forgotten and left outside of her life. When she brought that Christ consciousness back into the gates of her life, she found her life became happier, more productive, and full of possibilities.

Precognitive Dreams

Precognitive dreams refer to those nightly visions that seem to give you a peek into the future. An example is of one we sent to Rae the night before she was to give a lecture. She dreamed that the overhead projector would not work. In the dream we showed her looking at her reflection in a hotel-like restroom. There was a white substance all over her face. When she awoke, she interpreted the dream correctly to mean that she should check the overhead before her lecture, or she would end up with "egg on her face."

As we predicted, the hotel's projector would not work and when Rae asked for someone to fix it, no one was able to help her. Remembering the dream, she decided to make do without the visual aid of transparencies. During her lecture, a mechanic fixed the projector just as Rae was winding up her talk. We inspired her to use the transparencies as a summary. Afterward, a person complimented Rae, saying that he was most impressed with the calm and serenity she displayed when things went wrong. Silently, she thanked us for giving her a heads up in the dream the night before.

Past-Life Dreams

Lastly, we have shown a dream to Rae where she was sitting in a box seat to the left of a stage. Three women stood on the stage in front of the red velvet curtains facing away from her to her right. The first woman was a petite Italian who was singing her heart out. The second was a tall African American who was singing her heart out. The third was a petite Native American woman who was singing her heart out. Suddenly, the Italian took off her head and turned to hand it to the woman behind her who took off her head and handed it to the woman behind her.

End of dream.

Now, Rae found this dream rather bizarre, but in asking us what it was all about, we revealed the reason why she had not gone professional with her clear soprano voice as her instructor in college had suggested. It was because she had experienced three previous lifetimes as a singer. The exchanging of heads meant that they were her—all one and the same!

When we reveal past lives for clients, we explain why they might have phobias or why a certain person just seems to dislike them for no known reason. That person could be subconsciously remembering them as an enemy from another long-ago time.

Although this was a vision given during a session with one of Rae's clients, we share it with you to reveal another noteworthy past-life vision. In the beginning of her work with us, we inspired Rae to use a person's metal object such as a ring to make and energy contact with her client's spirit vibration so as to receive information from us. It is called psychometry. Yet for this client, we showed Rae how to use an amethyst stone rather than the person's metal object. We instructed her to have the client hold the root of the stone against her solar plexus while they chatted for a few moments. Then Rae was to take the stone and hold the points toward her solar plexus.

Immediately, we revealed to Rae the woman's past lifetime. We gave Rae a vivid movie-like picture of a young Arabian girl dancing before two older men within a large tent. They sat on red velvet cushions with gold tassels and admired the beauty of the young woman. When the dance ended, the girl threw her arms around the one man who was her father. When the father announced his child was to marry the old man next to him, the girl rebelled and declared she would never marry him because she was in love with the captain of the guards. The father insisted. The girl refused and dashed outside, leapt upon her stallion and fled off into the night.

Rae continued her vision of the young girl who ran straight into a warring party hiding a short distance away. They captured the girl and took her to their camp. After they realized who she was, they knew it was too dangerous for them to hold her captive. Instead, they stabbed her in the stomach…

Suddenly the client cried out in alarm and brought Rae out of her trance-like state. She learned the woman had been having recurring nightmares of someone stabbing in her stomach. The recurring dreams had caused her to become acrophobic. We reassured the client this violent experience would not happen again. We revealed this drama not just for the client's enlightenment and relief from troubling dreams, but for Rae to gain new gifts in her work with clients' dreams.

Dreams are the subject of many books where the author tries to interpret the signs and symbols often encountered in the dream world. As we suggested earlier, it is better for you to create your own dictionary of personal symbols, for these are the true reflections of your spirit's vocabulary. Your symbols will then be used for messages from your angel guides.

In this, we say—all things work for your greater good—especially dreams.

In another chapter, we will spend more time explaining how your brain brings visions that activate your imagination and offer you amazing insights.

But first, we need to discuss that burning question: Why are you here on Earth in the first place?

Chapter 9
What is My Purpose For Being Here?

Your purpose for being here is to KNOW YOURSELF! Begin now to clarify what you believe to be true.

Beloved soul! You do not know how powerful you are! Believe in yourself! To prove this, keep a daily record of your ideas and beliefs and what you did about them.

We do not make light of this: Your power is in your emotions! They are constantly creating your life. In order to bring forth an idea, you must trust and believe that you can make an abstract idea a reality.

In order to do this, you must raise your consciousness out of those negative emotions of anxiety, fear, anger, and frustration into a positive belief that all is possible. You must lift your heart and mind and soul into joyful emotions allowing you to imagine your desires becoming a reality within your world. This is only the first step...

Once you clasp an idea to your heart, you must hold it fast within your mind, become excited about it and constantly be open to new ideas as to what to do next to turn that abstract idea into a physical reality.

We have given the example earlier of how Rae created a beautiful rug without previous knowledge of the art form. We will always lead you to create whatever we place before you. We will never offer an idea without the means to achieve its goal.

When you are inspired to manifest an abstract idea, act upon it until a roadblock stops you. Then fill up your emotional fuel tank with determination to continue until you are successful. It may mean being patient while you wait for the next idea that moves you forward. It may mean researching everything you can about your desire. It may mean speaking to others who may have valuable input. It does mean patience and trust that the idea you have been given is for you to make a reality.

To discover your purpose for being on planet Earth at this moment in time, we suggest you begin by probing your desires and beliefs. Only through your belief system can you alone define what inspires you to create. You cannot even remember all the times you have created a solution to a problem or have been inspired to create something for someone just for fun or felt inspired to work on a project that would take a long-time commitment.

Think of one or two of those times now. Write down your accomplishments, your successes, your creations that were just for fun—and rejoice in them!

We suggest you spend an hour in meditation with pen and paper to sort through all the concepts you have about who or what God is; about the precepts of your religious background or lack of; everything about what you perceive as truth.

We repeat the suggestion that you keep a daily log of discoveries in how you create everyday events—good and bad—and your emotional reaction to them. This is not a diary of what you did that day. Rather, it is an accounting of how you reacted **emotionally** to the people and events you encountered throughout your day. As you uncover your negative thoughts and emotions, you can take the first step in eliminating them and thus become free to create a more prosperous and happy life.

You create the laws that govern your life to keep you safe and happy. Make a list of "Thou Shalt Nots" regarding your relationships. Where do you "draw the line?" What makes you angry? What hurts your feelings? Record all emotional reactions in order to learn each day's many purposes and how you are fulfilling them. When you study any encounters that break your "laws" you will begin to eliminate some and create new ones.

An accounting of your daily decisions is another way to become aware of your beliefs that then recreate your life.

While humankind has created more laws than one can count, God has only one law – the Law of Love. It supersedes all other commandments and spiritual laws relating to the evolution of the human spirit. Humans continue to create laws to serve the safety and justice of honest people against those who would serve their own selfish purposes.

Had it not been for the injustice done to Moses' people, there would not have been the Ten Commandments. These are still powerful guidelines for the soul on its journey through a foreign land. Moses' people had a need for a "real, solid, visible" God. It led them to create a false one. People are still creating false gods today in their worship of the body's beauty and their focus on prosperity and abundance through what money can buy.

Let us review Moses' ancient commandments with a fresh perspective from the soul's viewpoint. Remembering that Moses' story came when his people were driven out of Egypt to flee for their lives. Remember also, they followed a strict belief system with many rules and regulations. The gift of these simple commandments was to return Moses' people to those beliefs in the one God of their faith.

The Ten Commandments

1. I am the Lord thy God. Thou shalt have no other gods before me.

    For each person God becomes a personal deity who will inspire, uplift, and guide the person throughout their life. There are many names of God. Many beginner souls fear God and act out of that fear. God is pure energy and pure love. God sees you as perfect exactly as you are.

2. Thou shalt not take the name of the Lord thy God in vain.

    Reverence for the person's name for God can also be a means of condemning other names in a righteous belief their god is the only right god!

3. Remember to keep holy the Sabbath day.

    Every day is the Sabbath when the advanced soul realizes they are one with God and that God is everywhere and in everyone.

4. Honor thy father and thy mother.

    Being respectful of your parents even if you no longer follow their beliefs is to respect their gift of life to you. Sometimes this is not possible when the parents' commands are not in alignment with your soul's story. It takes great courage to go against the plans of your parents for you. It does not mean to abandon them in their time of need.

5. Thou shalt not commit murder.

Taking another's life in battle when it is either your life or another's is not murder. Taking a life for your personal gain is murder and may create a lifetime when your life may be taken in like manner. For each life seeks balance for your soul. God's law of Cause and Effect is simply the law of balance. Each soul will experience all things, all emotions and gain great wisdom from it all.

6. Thou shalt not commit adultery.

    Perhaps it might be better to say, "Thou shalt not break a promise." If you agreed to remain faithful "until death do you part," then the breaking of that vow can only be made at the mutual agreement between the partners. To break the vow without the partner's knowledge will bring about a great deal of grief and pain. And what you do unto others shall be done unto you as well.

7. Thou shalt not steal.

    Whatever you do to the least of God's creations you do unto God, for the Oneness shall not be ignored. Beginner souls who steal are always greatly surprised and indignant when someone steals from them. Lessons can be repeated many times in many lives before they are learned.

8. Thou shalt not bear false witness against thy neighbor.

    This covers the other commandments of honesty, integrity, compassion, and love. Lies about another will bounce back with lies made about you.

9. Thou shalt not covet thy neighbor's wife.

The pleasures of the flesh can lead to many kinds of negative results when indulged without concern for the ties that bind one to another. It can disrupt the body both emotionally and physically for disharmony creates internal negative emotions that can result in illness or in upheaval in one's outer world.

10. Thou shalt not covet thy neighbor's goods.

Envy toward another perhaps because you do not believe they deserve what they have acquired in physical treasures are emotions that disturb the body's energy and can lead to a disruption in the body's health or in the life's flow of positive experiences.

What are your commandments? What are the rules your soul follows throughout your life? How do these rules serve your purpose for being here on planet Earth? How do they make you happy? How do they keep you content? Or how do they lead you into uncomfortable dramas that drain your emotional energy?

By keeping a daily log of your responses to each emotional expression and who, what or how it was triggered, you will gain more power over the direction of your life to bring about more happy resolutions to problems and more creations that will delight and please you.

Open your mind, dear one to who and what makes you happy—and discover who and what makes you unhappy. Once you begin to awaken to how your life evolves through your decisions made from your emotional responses, you will be halfway home.

In our next chapter, we will answer your questions about how to be happy—an excellent topic of discussion.

Chapter 10
How Can I Be Happy When...?

...the world is in such a mess?...when my loved one just died?...when I'm in pain?...when...?

We say unto you: Raise Your Consciousness!

You can never be completely happy if you always find something or someone who disrupts your view of happiness. When you say, "How can I be happy when..." When what? When someone is in your way? When people always challenge your happiness? When people disappoint you, confront you, argue with you, or betray you?

Your purpose while in this world is to rediscover God <u>through</u> people! As you come to know, love and serve humanity, you will find the indwelling of divinity within yourself. To do this, you must raise your consciousness out of fear and doubt, anxiety and anger into the light of truth to trust in your own dear self and God. We speak of raising your emotional energy tank out of the emptiness of negative emotions and into positive, mindful energy vibrations.

Spiritual consciousness reflects your soul's level of awareness of God's laws. Obviously, beginner souls have little knowledge of any laws. They can only learn of them when they break a law and experience an uncomfortable response. If they knowingly break a law and do not receive a consequence, they will continue to break laws. Only from a moment to moment **conscious awareness** to connect the act with the experience of an uncomfortable result can the soul learn how to navigate within a physical world filled with laws.

Now, here you are, dear reader, on your planet where you cannot escape the lower levels of emotions. Even after having had many lifetimes of consciousness-training, you may still have anxieties and doubts and fears that crop up to muddy your perception of life on Earth. These are your challenges to living a happy life. By simply recognizing your fears with the determination to eliminate them, you will raise your consciousness into peace and joy.

Imagine you could take a consciousness shower. When you wash out the grit of fear and doubt from your mind and emotions, you will automatically raise your spirit's consciousness. You will sparkle with a new awareness of eternal love. You will begin to glow. Your light will inspire others to wash their gritty concepts, too. Sooner rather than later, the raising of consciousness will spill over into your personal world of family and friends—much like the story of the 100th monkey.

Negative people will either raise their consciousness to become brighter, happier individuals or they will seem to fade from your life. And soon, your light will spread throughout the world and you will see people awakening all over the globe.

When you demonstrate humor, peace, harmony, integrity, and joy within yourself, you help everyone around you raise their consciousness to do the same. God designed you to bring Its divine light into your physical world. When you do, you bring joy into the lives of all the people around you <u>by simply glowing</u>.

When you raise your consciousness, many good things start to happen:

- Your perception becomes wider so you can begin to see the bigger picture.

- Your intuition sharpens as you become aware of your soul sending new ideas for solving everyday problems.

- Inner visions supply you with ideas where your welfare is concerned: what your body needs to be healthy for example.

- You develop a sense of knowing how to live a happier, more joy-filled life.

- You will increase your awareness of the subtle energies around you and others.

- You will stay balanced during stressful times.

- You will have an increased awareness of your soul's purpose for your life.

- You will have a driving need to increase beauty and goodness in your life by beautifying your mind and your surroundings.

- You will experience a great thirst for knowledge and be led to find answers to long-held questions.

- A higher sense of integrity will grow within you. It will not allow you to be dishonest with anyone in any way, especially with yourself.

- You will increase your sense of compassion and tolerance toward others, making it easier to accept them exactly as they are without trying to change them, thus making detachment easier and confrontations less frequent.

- You will have an increased confidence in decision-making that will lead to better choices with results that are more of your choosing.

- Creative ideas will "pop!" along with a strong willpower to follow through with them.

- Relationships will either strengthen or dissolve.

- Your energy will increase, giving you time to do more things of your choosing.

Scientists continue to study where consciousness resides within the human body. They conduct brain research and look everywhere. They will not find it because your consciousness resides with your invisible spirit. Some scientists are reluctantly coming to that conclusion. It will begin the merging of science with the non-physical worlds. In fact, it has already begun.

Throughout this book, we have been presenting a picture of you in bits and pieces like a huge jig-saw puzzle of how as humans you navigate within a complex, time-trapped world. We ask you to bear with us on our next conceptual ride as we describe those invisible, amazing, powerful, life-changing energy orbs of light residing right within your physical and spirit bodies.

We described these orbs of light earlier in Chapter 6. They are also the receptors of your consciousness. When they are bright and polished, you are as well. When they are depleted and dull, so, too, are you.

With this knowledge—perhaps not new to many of you, but hopefully with a different perspective and a greater respect for your vehicle of expression—you will more easily awaken to your spirit with a sense of inner peace and joy, thus raising your consciousness into an advanced awareness—from an eagle's eye view.

Again, we emphasize the use of a scientific journal to record your experiments within your world. How often do you fall into negative emotions? What are the results of your experiments because of it? How did you change your mind and decide to use more positive emotions to bring forth new ideas? How did that change the results of your experiments?

It is wise to carry a small notebook to record those flashes of ideas that often come when least expected as in driving or just before you fall asleep. Be sure to jot them down as they can easily disappear from your memory just like dreams.

We often send new problem-solving ideas just before sleep. We will present ways to attain that state through meditations in later chapters. This will unlock many doors for you.

Chapter 11
What About My Work And Career?

When you love your work, it becomes fulfilling and meaningful. When you hate your work, you are denying your soul's need for fulfilling the divine plan for your life.

Too many people work paycheck-to-paycheck, holding on out of fear they will not be able to pay their bills. Often, people put up with undesirable work conditions or inadequate pay out of that desperation to have an income—any kind of income. It is admirable that they would stick with it for as long as they do. It is sad they do not know how to create a better work life.

How <u>do</u> I create a better work life?

Study this book as we present many ways to have **all your needs met each day of your life**. Start this moment by repeating the previous sentence several times a day, every day, and hold in your heart the certainty that it is possible and doable. This is called an "Affirmation" and although it may seem like being a bit of a fool to speak such ideas, hold fast to the knowledge that you are a co-creator with God and it is your job to learn to do just that—create!

We caution you to be realistic...do not immediately repeat over and over, "I will win the lottery!" Only if such a thing is for your highest good and is part of God's plan for your life will such a windfall occur.

Your soul does have the entire life mapped out for you. It will offer many adventures and millions of choices before you are ready to leave your world for the next.

How do I find the perfect job for me?

Follow the divine inspiration given to you each day. Learn to listen inwardly and not depend entirely upon what the world has to say to you. Do listen to the advice of others who have knowledge. For example, if you might wish to explore a career as a veterinarian, obtain a job working for one, being willing to clean out cages, assist with the paperwork, and even be allowed to help with surgery as Rae's daughter did. She had bought a horse and needed the services of a vet. She worked in the profession long enough to decide it was not for her.

She chose to become an Occupational Therapist and eventually gained a Doctorate degree in her field.

Rae will share with you how we inspired her to solve a seemingly unsolvable problem of teaching grammar during her work with eighth-grade Language Arts students. They expressed their hatred of her class and of grammar.

I searched for a way to impress upon my students the need for English grammar. Raphael inspired me to begin with having them imagine they had to find a job. I assigned my students to obtain one application form. One brought in a half page form from a gas station. Another student brought one from a bank that was eight pages long.

I invited a bank manager to speak to my students who learned that their application would be "deep sixed" if they left anything blank.

My students studied the abbreviations in want ads.

Then, Raphael inspired me to set up my students into groups where they were to form a company with the objective of hiring people to fill positions in their company. As expected, the academics grouped together and the "Goof-offs" thought this was going to be easy. Each student was given a second role of finding a job in someone else's company. With five English classes, I gave each student a five-digit number for identification.

We studied application forms. Then, each group was told to create an application form for their company. I did not correct their grammar. After I made copies of the applications, the students were not allowed to make any corrections.

The objective of this "Job Search Game" was to experience the consequences of their choices and how studying English might help them obtain a job.

It was a pass/fail assignment. Each company had to fill their job openings. Each student had to be hired into another's company that was not in their own classroom.

The game grew exciting whenever anyone found a grammatical error because they could charge the applicant or the job managers a fee for each grammatical error found. Since the company could do nothing to erase their errors, they were stuck with the loss of income.

The students learned how to create a "Letter of Inquiry" and again they were charged by the company if they made any grammatical errors.

The game was wildly successful, with students finding out the hard way what it would cost them to make grammatical errors! Although the only grade given was Pass/Fail, it was a great motivator for each company to fill its required hires and for each person to get hired and to seek the reward offered for the richest student at the end of the game.

One brilliant student who knew he would have no problem passing the grammatical hurdle, only filled out one application form. On it the company asked about his hobbies. He wrote, "Making mud pies." They sent him a rejection letter, saying he wasn't serious enough to be hired into their company. It astounded him especially because the deadline for getting a job was fast approaching. The young man quickly wrote out several application forms and sent them out. He was accepted into a company just in the nick of time.

The boy commented to me afterwards that he'd never worked so hard in his English class. He also claimed that he never before had had so much fun.

Raphael brought to me a fellow teacher who encouraged me to send the game to a publisher, and it was published as Exciting Language Arts Projects" in 1984 by J. Weston Walch, Publisher, Portland, Main 04104-0658 under my name then as Betty Brisse Sullivan. It is no longer in print but may be resurrected if enough people ask for it.

We do not seek to promote Rae's work, for she has long ago retired from public life. We give examples of how these ideas presented can work for those of you willing to study and learn how to incorporate them within your own life story.

Dear reader, we present these examples of Rae's life to encourage you to follow the inspirations of your angels and guides throughout your life. We are waiting to help you fill all your needs. Because Rae has learned how to listen to our suggestions many miracles have seemed to happen. They will do so with you as well. Trust in miracles. Trust in your own inner guidance.

What about fame and fortune?

All things are possible while exploring your physical world.

A desire to express the soul through using a talent that could bring about fame and fortune is a wonderful challenge that reaps many rewards—and many challenges.

Study any famous person and you will agree this is so. When dealing with money and power, you will be led to those who abuse it for their own selfish ends that can result in pain and suffering for many talented and naïve seekers.

And yet, we remind you that your life is built upon a plan that will balance previous life experiences, often bringing in people who will both help and exploit you in this present-day life story.

You and your Council have set up the actors from previous stories who will play the roles of support teams and antagonists. No story would be worth expressing without all the elements of good story-telling: an interesting and compelling main character who grows from the experience (you), a support team to encourage you to persist when you want to give up—your friends and support group; and challenges that will help you rise above it all and succeed—your naysayers and the people who latch onto the tail of your ascending stardom.

We suggest you study the lives of the kind of famous people you wish to emulate. Become aware of their challenges:

betrayal from those they trusted; exposure to drugs and escape mechanisms, relationships that may be only passing but can be heart-breaking.

Most importantly, find people who will believe in you and support your visions for success.

Chapter 12
What About Relationships?

Relationships act as mirrors for you to discover who you are. They hand you many golden keys to unlock God's wisdom and reveal your soul.

A Soul's Role in Group Relationships

In every group, individuals assume a role according to their soul's color vibration and their soul's maturity. This brings to the group a unique dynamism that blends, enhances and energizes everyone...or detracts, distracts, drains and scatters energy. Yet, each group serves as an opportunity to raise consciousness by challenging you to grow in patience, compassion, wisdom, and love.

1. **The red soul** will always try to assume leadership, saying something like, "We'll meet once a week on Thursday afternoons." If positive, this person brings all viewpoints forward and stays neutral. If negative, this person may become a tyrant who insists that things be done his/her way.

2. Without even asking, **the orange soul** may be given leadership over the red soul's bid for it. People will vote this person in over a young red soul who is looking for power and control. But since orange souls are very few and far between, you do not see them too often.

3. **The yellow soul** is a fact-gatherer. It might say, "I'll look that up online and get the information for you."

4. **The green soul** will offer to bring the refreshments or to take the minutes for the meeting. This person is likely to say, "Can I get you anything while I'm up?"

5. **The blue soul** will brainstorm, saying perhaps, "We can call... and they'll do it. Or we can..." They may be the person who designs the fliers or advertising.

6. **The indigo soul** will be the one who says, "We need to make a statement of intention and our purpose for doing it." This soul can also be the antagonist of the group in looking for the downside of a situation or it may seek to find which obstacles might occur down the road. Neither of these actions are negative.

7. **The violet soul** will reach for the stars, saying something like, "Wouldn't it be great if..." or "I think we should begin with a prayer."

In intimate relationships between two people, all these roles are expressed in the same manner, depending upon the vibrational color of the souls and more importantly, the experience or soul development of each partner.

For example, red souls often partner with a green soul who will support them. Two red souls may create conflict, especially if one soul has had very few lifetimes of experience in dealing with relationships. That person may feel insecure and too needy and thus cause the stronger partner to lose interest.

You can tell the development of a person's soul by listening to their conversation. Does the person continually turn the conversation back to his/herself? Does the person interrupt you to give an opinion or worse still, to chide you for your ideas? Is the person immediately interested in a physical experience with you? If you answered yes, most likely that person is still in the beginning stages of sentient life on your planet and is mainly interested in figuring out what he/she believes. If a person truly hears what you have to say, then he/she has been here many times and is a mature soul with whom you would be comfortable speaking of your innermost ideas and beliefs. He/she will be equally interested in getting to know you—your likes, dislikes, beliefs and fears?

Your greatest challenge is to get to know yourself by listening to your self-talk. Again, we encourage you to keep a daily log of your emotions as they relate to decisions made. Root out those negative subconscious beliefs that keep you spinning in circles. Delve deeper and deeper into the discovery of who you are until you touch your soul. Then—and only then—will you be ready for that perfect relationship. As you raise your consciousness your aura begins to expand and glow, attracting many to you, especially a person who has also raised his/her consciousness.

Needy people with their unrealistic expectations of you can bring out your compassion or your anger. They can either demand your attention thus causing you to cower or they can be a catalyst to push you to stand up for yourself.

Where is My Soulmate?

This is the question we are asked most often when people come to us for a consultation. They are looking for that perfect partner they believe will bring them happiness and bliss—and solve all their problems. Unfortunately, not too many people have obtained that goal even if they did find their soulmate. More often, people are searching for someone to take care of them financially or emotionally—or both—and when that doesn't work, they end up being alone again.

Your soulmates (yes—plural) are all vibrating at the same energy frequency. You study together and discuss your experiences within the planet's physical dimension of time and space. Your soulmates most often play a supporting role during your story.

Therefore, relationships outside of your soul group will better challenge you to new heights of wisdom.

When souls separate themselves from the oneness of God by incarnating within the physical dimension, they experience loneliness. They feel stuck within the elements of time and space. This drives them to find a companion—a soulmate—when they are really searching for God to complete them. We have said that you are One with God. Only when you truly believe this and can feel it throughout your entire body can you become completely whole again. No human partner can give you that feeling of completion.

Your true soulmates rarely partner with you since you live with them in the soul realm. While there, you do not have to deal with the human emotions of physical love, anger, frustration, or hate. You are more like classmates for the purpose of seeking knowledge. Your soulmates simply know you too well and, therefore, they would not be a challenge for you or for them to couple with you in a love relationship within the physical world. Although soulmates can, of course, be attracted to one another.

The purpose for the soul's incarnation is always the seeking of new knowledge in the art of manifesting within the physical dimension and in so doing becoming one again with God.

Unaware of this, human individuals continue to search for that perfect mate not realizing that **they are really searching to create a balance of the male/female, positive/negative aspects <u>within themselves.</u>** They may seek to find this in another, but they cannot until they reconnect with their soul and with God as their One Mate—the Creator of all that is.

Mission Mates

What may seem to be a love relationship could also be a mission mate whose intense interest in a goal or a mission will bring people together. Their passion for the vision may create a physical attraction leading to a sexual commitment to one another.

Because of a project they had agreed to work on together before the life began, they may give more power to it being a soul partnership than it really is. This like-mindedness can lead to an intimate relationship but more because of the project than the mate-for-life purpose. When the project is completed, the intimacy of the relationship can dwindle and the people may go separate ways.

The Five Criteria for a Compatible Love Relationship

Most humans put the exploration of physical compatibility first when it needs to be last.

Notice how all the internet matchmaking companies first show a picture of the person, making physical appearance the first criteria in choosing someone for a relationship. They may have a long list of personality characteristics for you to complete, but that photo can be the door to unlock your potential mate and if you are not beautiful, well, it could slam the door tightly shut. It has motivated some people to either refuse to show a picture or to put someone else's picture in their place.

Observe the millions of dollars spent on commercials that stress physical beauty. They suggest that long lashes will lure your soulmate. Diet commercials suggest how fast you can lose that fat— suggesting you could never find your soulmate unless you do.

We say to you, dear reader, your physical appearance, while important to you, is simply not the most important part in a relationship.

Rae had a client who was close to being obese and yet, she outlived three husbands, saying the last was the best. Her generous heart, pleasing personality, intellectual wit and humor outshone her physical appearance as judged by young souls.

Intimate relationships are a highway to God.

While all relationships offer a peek at God, intimate relationships open the door to emotions otherwise not explored. And, again, we emphasize how your emotions are at the core of everything you manifest in your physical dimension.

When you explore a physical relationship leading to childbearing and raising children, you will find your true understanding of the values you hold and wish to share with another close to you. You will constantly be challenged in those beliefs and in your ability to speak as an authority regarding them.

Expectations can be the death of a relationship.

Intimate relationships offer a clear reflection of your innermost self for we say unto you each relationship will become a mirror to you. When you choose to praise or condemn, look within. What you see in a beloved, you must first become aware of it within yourself. The saying, "It takes one to know one," can become brutally true when finding it within yourself. For truly you could not have recognized it within another.

While it becomes a natural progression of events that lead to these expectations, become aware of them even before you look for an intimate relationship.

Make a list of the qualities you seek in a mate. Often, the person's physical attributes make the top of the list. They are false values. Look again.

We suggest you study our five criteria below in creating a happy union and then make it your list of what you seek in a mate.

Five Criteria for a Happy Relationship

1: Compatibility of Soul Vibrations

Remember, compatibility is mostly about a revisiting of situations yet unresolved or reuniting with a soul where you had a pleasant encounter. You rarely interact with a new soul. You may think, "It was love at first sight," and most likely that is because you have known them in a previous lifetime

Often, although you may have met them before, it was your Council of Elders that put blinders on you and totally erased any negative memory when the union is for your soul's growth. There are many reasons why two people come together in a love relationship—and it is not always to create a "happily ever after."

In 1989, Rae had been divorced for two years when she came back into contact with a choral student she had had in 1956 during her first year of teaching. Fern...her real name...had been a problem student, always getting into trouble for smoking or truancy. She attached herself to Rae who became her mentor.

Then, fast forward to 1989, two years after Rae's divorce from a thirty-two-year marriage, when we brought back this student to introduce Rae to her second husband, a widower of eight years.

Fern asked Rae for a picture of herself and said she knew of someone Rae needed to meet. When Bill (not his real name) received the picture, he ignored it because Rae's student was still a wildly individual character. Still, a few weeks later, he called, they met, and six months later they were married.

Although you would not call us matchmakers, we are.

Now, some would say Bill was Rae's Soulmate because they had such a compatible, loving relationship. But he was not. He was an advanced red soul who was used to being in charge and in control and yet he was never demanding of Rae and never tried to control her. He accepted her as she was and honored that. He loved her unconditionally.

Before their coming together, neither one of them had had unconditional love in a relationship. Too often, Bill had met women who sought his company because they knew he had his own home and was financially comfortable. They wanted someone to take care of them financially.

It never even entered Rae's mind to pursue him. In fact, we know it was one reason he was interested in her. He knew she was not playing hard to get and found it refreshing. Rae had just started dating others and told him she wanted to continue to do so.

Because Rae was able to listen to our guidance, she knew when Bill entered her life he was different. Although she resisted making any commitment to him, he recognized Rae as a partner he desired. When he realized she was dating other men, he gave her an ultimatum that forced Rae to make the decision to commit to him.

Start now really looking at your story as if you were to write your memoirs. What would you say about your life, about how certain events moved you in a different direction than you had planned, about how you were influenced by some great and wise people, and perhaps deceived by some young soul or two?

Have you had an experience with a baby soul who sought only his/her own needs? Has a partner become too dependent upon you for their emotional or financial support?

If you became dependent upon another for your needs to be filled, what would you do if that relationship ended? Or if it were in the reverse, where someone became too dependent upon you to meet their needs and it became too heavy a responsibility to bear, would you end the relationship?

Can you see how seeking a mate to fulfill your needs can be an error in judgment? **It is your responsibility to take care of your personal emotional and financial needs.**

If one person's soul is older and wiser, the partner may feel inferior. In order to feel superior, the partner may begin finding fault, making criticisms, and thus weakening the fabric of the relationship. When a partner is always finding fault with whatever you do, this may eventually drive you to consider ending the relationship.

Soul incompatibility can happen when two people seal the bond with a compromise in religious beliefs. For example, one partner may give up his religious beliefs to please another. Long-held beliefs do not go away easily. Some are cemented in the subconscious and will rear its head up when there is a conflict between the person and his soul or between the beliefs to be handed down to the couple's children.

A difference in political views is not as disruptive as spiritual differences. Although both can evoke great emotional responses, political views can be ignored but religious or spiritual beliefs come from the soul and mean a great deal more to the individual.

Another common thing we see now more than ever is a relationship where one person seeks to raise his/her consciousness while the other does not. The person expanding their awareness may eagerly try to share their new insights with the partner. If the partner is receptive and open to the new ideas, it can help the relationship grow. But if the partner is not interested and may indeed be intimidated by it, the relationship may be heading for trouble.

Soul age can be a key point in creating a good relationship. If one has a mature soul and the other is still young in experiences within the physical, there may be difficulties. The younger soul may express much more fear and use game playing to have his/her needs met.

Most green souls who need to nurture and mother may find a baby soul quite to their liking. In fact, green souls can blend well with almost every soul color. Only in soul maturity can an older green soul grow impatient and seek relief by leaving the relationship.

Most often, it is not the soul's color you are trying to match so much as it is the soul's age, which means how mature the soul has become.

In addition to what we have said about soul age in an earlier chapter, one quick way to discover the person's soul maturity is to watch how often the person blames others or life in general for any mistakes or problems they experience. If they are into that Blame Game, they are not a mature soul. Another sign of an immature soul is someone who always brings the conversation back to him or herself. (We discuss these "Games" in greater detail in the next chapter).

If you are reading this book, you are not a beginner soul, dear one! Beginner souls will be attracted **to you**. If you choose a partner who is seeking your wisdom and truth, you may find it a compatible relationship. If they are seeking to dominate you, to question and challenge you, again it could be for your own soul growth.

All relationships are a gift from God!

2: Intellectual Compatibility

Intellectual compatibility can be easily misunderstood. Intelligence does not necessarily equate with college degrees. Rae's first husband had two master's degrees and was extremely intelligent. She was a teacher with one master's degree, but they were not compatible.

Although her second husband had only a high school diploma, he had taken an apprenticeship in the trades and became highly sought after by large companies. His education also came from having had a variety of jobs throughout his life. Despite this, Bill felt his intellect was inferior to Rae with her degrees. They had many debates on the subject.

Education is not a measure of intelligence. When a couple can enjoy a lively two-sided conversation, when they have similar interests, when they can enjoy one another's company without speaking a word, and when they can feel safe to expose their souls to one another, then they are richly blessed with a compatible relationship.

3: Emotional Compatibility

It is not the beauty of the physical body that attracts a mate. It is your emotions being expressed in an aura of bright light that attracts another. If you have a sunny personality, others will be attracted to you no matter what your physical body may present.

Emotions play a big part in relationships. They say opposites attract, and perhaps that refers to emotions. If someone is depressed, they look for a partner who will pick them up. If someone is fearful and shy, they will seek to balance with someone who is brave and outgoing.

On the other hand, when you find someone who clicks with you emotionally because they have the same fears or the same doubts, sometimes that will be the mirror to awaken you to how you are living a life of disharmony and choose to do something different. This then would be a blessing.

Not many humans know how to love unconditionally. They cannot help putting some expectations upon you. Yet, unconditional love is what each person yearns for, what each person must strive to achieve first for themselves and then toward others. In expressing unconditional love, you glimpse the wondrous love that God has for you. Only then will you begin to understand your oneness with the Creator.

It goes without saying if you have a sour outlook on life, or if you are always taking the role of a cynic, your aura may be gloomy and dark and other people will sense that dark aura and steer clear of you.

4: Physical Compatibility

You may agree that getting to know the inner person is most important, but it is only natural that you may want a beautiful body to attract a mate. Birds wear bright colors. It inspires you to wear beautiful clothes and sweet perfume to be pleasing to someone special.

Yet, in your world today, the physical body is worshiped as a false god. Although it is merely a costume the soul wears for the brief run of their drama on Earth, it can become an obsession and a trap slowing down spiritual growth. Indeed, do take good care of the body, feed and water it carefully, enhance it with adornments, **but do not worship it.**

Unfortunately, the focus of attention on your physical bodies is what you have been taught to do. The commercials on television, billboards, radio, and everywhere encourage you to worry about your appearance, to believe it is all you must have to attract a soulmate. You have beauty competitions that turn little children into winners or losers. You are told to focus on clothes as a necessity to move up the corporate ladder and become a success. Do not be fooled. It is not your outer appearance but your soul that shines through and makes the biggest impressions. Trust this.

Your world reveres life in the physical above its soul. Because most souls on your planet are either beginner or intermediate souls, they are more concerned about gaining as much pleasure and success as possible before they die. Death becomes a taboo word, ignored for as long as possible, and often feared. This reflects the denial of the soul.

The soul's choice of the physical body's DNA serves a large purpose for the life. Red souls will desire a strong body, capable of physical feats. It would be most comfortable with another soul who enjoys jogging, mountain climbing, sports, and other strenuous activities.

Orange souls would gravitate toward green or blue souls who would be the emotional and spiritual helpmate to them.

Since yellow souls gravitate to quiet activities such as books, science or mathematics, their helpmate would tend toward another in their professional spear of influence. But again, green souls would make a dominant yellow soul very comfortable.

A blue soul is more inactive physically, enjoying creative activities that do not require use of the physical body. They would gravitate to other blue souls who like to read, converse, write or who are active in the arts. Red souls who enjoy music and the arts would also make good companions for blue souls.

Again, green souls can bridge the gap for any other soul color and be a compatible companion.

Indigo souls would seek another indigo that can see the bigger picture while also thinking out of the box. Intelligence would also be large criteria for compatibility. They would be most comfortable with an old red soul, or a yellow soul whose work would make them a helpmate.

A violet soul needs a green soul to be their mate in their desire to save souls. It needs someone who is of like mind spiritually as well as attractive physically as they may have a very public life.

Each person brings to a relationship all kinds of life experiences that make them uniquely who they are. Any union with another soul offers a wonderful opportunity to work through negative experiences and heal them. And yet, if that is why a person entered into a relationship—to have their partner heal them—then there may be trouble. No amount of physical touching, sexual compatibility or anything physical can heal the soul. That is each individual's personal journey. One can only look for support and compassion from their partner.

The physical compatibility includes mutual pleasure in joining two bodies in the sexual act. This is often where the soul will seek to overcome previous unfortunate experiences that left the person traumatized. For example, if a soul experienced a brutal rape in one lifetime, they might be sexually inhibited in this one. And, indeed, if the person experienced this in the present lifetime, then the union may have some difficulties.

Balance is the answer. Through a soul's many lifetimes of experiencing all kinds of relationships, it will raise its consciousness and speed the soul's growth in gaining wisdom and divine knowledge.

5: Intimacy & Trust

This last gauge of a thriving relationship is likely the most important, for when there is intimacy and trust between two people both inside and outside of the bedroom, the relationship will blossom into sheer joy. That trust is built over time in the courtship period. It needs to be nourished after a commitment has been made. Trust is nourished by sharing the silly things you do, by being able to laugh at yourself with your mate and know it will not be used against you later.

LGBTQ Relationships

You have heard us say over and over that there is never any judgment from God or from the angels regarding a soul's experimentation within a physical dimension. The divine plan for each soul's life is masterfully unfolding each moment. The intimacy of knowing the soul with such gentle patience and love can only bring goodness and joy for the individual.

The need for a mate will awaken within the soul a drive to find its complement regardless of sexual orientation. When soul's meet it is the heart that cements the relationship not the sexual drive. It is often a previous life recognition that sees the soul rather than the physical person.

Same-sex relationships are a natural order of things when past life loves return. The attraction is instant. They became blind to the physical person being of the same sex.

Usually, one of the same-sex partners will play the male dominant role, while the other will play the supporting role. This, again, can echo their previous lifetime together when they were in male and female bodies.

Again, we say: when you raise your consciousness high above the earthy perspective and see from the soul's experiences of having played both sexes more than once, then perhaps you can see more clearly why God does not judge.

If a soul has chosen predominantly male roles for many lifetimes, their Council may suggest they choose a female body in the next incarnation. But when the soul arrives on the planet in this foreign body, it may still think of itself as male and will be attracted to female bodies and thus same-sex relationship will seem more of the natural order for them. This same is true in the reverse. If a soul has been predominantly female in the past several lifetimes and finds itself in a male body, it most likely will be attracted to other male bodies.

Consider all these complex factors that are far beyond the understanding of most humans on the planet. Only then you can begin to comprehend God's magnificent plan for the education of souls as explorers of physical worlds. You may also come to appreciate how God does not judge anyone.

Chapter 13
How Do I Win At Life's Games?

Ah, dear souls! Truly, life is a game and Earth is your game-board. The players are all the people who are in your life now or may be in your future. Each experience with a new player opens a whole new chapter in your soul's story.

We encourage you to welcome and embrace every person who enters your stage on Earth. Although they may seem like a new acquaintance, they may be old soul friends who have gifts to share with you. They are an opportunity to move your soul one step closer to winning at your Game of Life.

When your first impression of a stranger arouses caution, anxiety, fear or mistrust...listen to your inner senses. Move with awareness while in their presence. They may be presenting a false face. They may have been an enemy in a previous lifetime where they may have betrayed you in some way. The emotional scar can fester and itch and awaken. Flair-ups of anger toward you for no reason may be triggered by these buried animosities.

Finely tune your senses to receive intuitive responses. But do not allow the negative energy between you to cause you to move backwards on your game board. Instead, greet the new player with openness and kindness, offering trust with a measure of caution. In this, you take a quantum leap forward—even if this new acquaintance may turn out to prove your caution was accurate. On the other hand, allow for the possibility that perhaps the past lifetime rival or enemy has gained soul growth and sought you out to mend emotional discord.

We say unto you, rejoice and be glad in all the players on your game board for they have been precisely chosen by God to appear at this moment in time to speed your awakening.

We shall examine the emotional games people can play as they enter your game board. Become aware that sentient life is only a game as each actor moves with you until they leave your life for one reason or another. Let us explore the ways they may play a role as challengers on your game board. And then we will suggest counter moves for you to always be a winner at your Game of Life.

Or they may put it more bluntly and say, "It's all your fault that this happened."

The Blame Game

These are people who use you as an excuse for their actions or mistakes. You'll hear them saying, "If you hadn't done this, then this would not have happened, and I wouldn't have done that."

Beware! You have entered the Blame Game which can throw you directly into the Guilt Game. These are games played mostly by younger, less experienced souls. They have not yet learned the law of cause and effect. It has been said that what goes out comes back. It is like a boomerang. When you send out loving, compassionate thoughts, it comes back like a kiss on the cheek. But when you send out vindictive, blaming thoughts, it can come back to you with unpleasant experiences

Players of the Blame Game believe that things happen **to them**, that life is created from the outside world ~ inward, like everyone is out to get them. The truth is: **Life is created from within ~ outward.** Your fears and beliefs are always being challenged. New knowledge and wisdom lead you to become the winner of your game.

A beginner soul's focus is on the small radius of their own space within their own emotions and thoughts. They rarely see anyone but themselves even as they look into the mirror of another's eyes.

These souls blame the world for their mistakes or call it bad luck instead of having the wisdom to know the energy of each thought, each emotion, each intention is sent into the individual's world of energy to bring back experiences of like kind. When a spirit plays the Blame Game, they are seeing life from a victim's perspective because they believe they have no control over their lives.

Remember, dear souls, you are divinely guided and protected by your guardian angel. Every kind thought you have for others, every loving emotion you express can be a smart move forward on your game board. Anything else can be a step backward.

Intent is the key thing here. **If you had no intent to do harm to another** but something happened when the offended person believes you are to blame, then there is no blame or even a need for an apology on your part.

But if you deliberately offended another **with malice of intent,** then repercussions may send you directly to Jail and you are told, "Do not pass Go!"

Also consider that perhaps that grave misunderstanding that caused the end to a friendship might have been for your greatest good. The situation could have been set up by your Council of Elders to allow the dissolution of a relationship that was no longer serving your soul's development.

The Entitlement Game

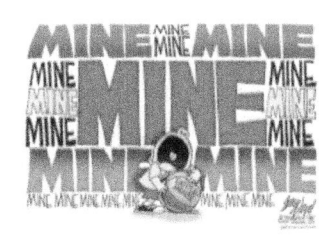

Of course, you must be aware of those who have an Entitlement Complex. Many young people born of privilege can be influenced to enter this game. If they do something wrong or even with malicious intent, they know their wealth or influence will get them out of the consequences of their actions. Many who play this game believe they have a right to be happy which means they can do whatever is necessary or take what they need regardless of the consequences. These are young souls who have no regard for the rights of others. They see themselves as above the law because of their power and influence.

Again, we point out the development of this soul comes through the consequences of its choices while in the physical world. These young souls have a lot of expectations that others will always take care of them.

Many marriages are created from the need of one person seeking a caregiver in another. The need to be rescued from poverty or from a previous relationship gone bad causes them to enter the game board. When another person steps upon their game board to rescue them, expectations can enslave both to an endless game.

To win at this game, we say yet again: You are the creator of your world. This game may send surprises to challenge you, but how you respond to them is entirely your move upon your game board.

You may think you have to do this all by yourself. You do not. Whenever you become uncomfortable with another player on your Earth's stage, look to see what game you are both playing. **Avoid expectations of the other person to behave in the way you would.** If the person's soul is not as advanced as yours, your disappointment will be the end game.

The Guilt Trip Game

Every soul who has stepped onto Earth's stage knows about guilt trips either from being the brunt of them or from being the perpetrator of them. Parents often use this technique to get their children to do what they want them to do. Love is the fruit of this forbidden tree when a player says, "If you loved me you would..." Or... "If you are loyal to me, you will do this for me."

While it is important to avoid putting expectations on others, you cannot allow others to put expectations upon you.

Many souls are not even aware of another's expectations imposed upon them as they have fallen into the game of so needing others approval and love that they give up their personal needs to fulfill those of the other.

Listen to your inner senses that warn you when something is not comfortable for you. And then take steps to honor your inner guidance that is God speaking to you through your spirit self. Listen and heed your needs when you are tempted to ignore them in order to please another.

When someone wants you to rescue them or do something you do not feel comfortable doing, simply say, "No thank you." Or… "That isn't comfortable for me right now," or "Let me think (pray) about it. I'll get back to you." And then…do not get back to them!

The Self-Pity Game

The "Poor Me" game is played by people who are convinced that life is determined to mow them down and trample them under. This is another form of the Victim Complex.

Again, we say that inexperienced souls may accuse you of not appreciating them for all the good things they do for you. They may berate you for daring to expect them to help you when you are feeling overwhelmed or overburdened. They let you know how much they are overworked and overburdened already. They wear a sign that says, "Poor me! Poor me! Poor me!"

To give a baby soul the pity it seeks will only make it crave more. Babies learn that when they cry, mother will come running. The people who play this game have learned that when they cry for help, no one can refuse them, and they actually come to believe they cannot do anything for themselves. If you were to put expectations upon them, they may feel used and abused. Perhaps a few more lifetimes will allow them to overcome this need.

Therefore, we have no suggestions as to how to help a person filled with self-pity. It is best to change the subject or walk away.

The Game of "But I only want you to be happy!"

There are constant worriers. They say that they love you so much and want you to be happy that they cannot help themselves in trying to convince you to do things their way as they certainly know what is best for you. They try to interfere in your life with their good-hearted suggestions or unsolicited help. These are the parents who continuously bail out their children from their misdeeds or mistakes. They may be overprotective and never allow their children to experience the consequences of their actions and thus learn the valuable information gained from the experience.

Wanting someone to be happy is an impossible task. Perhaps you may desire this so you can stop worrying about them or because you still need to control them for your own happiness. How can you know what will make another happy when most often you do not know how to be happy yourself?

People who play this game are chronic worriers. They can imagine all kinds of terrible things happening to their loved ones. Please remember: **Worry is negative energy. It drags you down. Whenever you worry about another, you drag them down!**

Divine energy constantly flows around and through you. When a wave of worry rushes through, fragments of another's thoughts might be the trigger. It may make you itch. Do not scratch! Instead, transform any negative wave into a rush of positive, uplifting energy and send it right back to the person who rose in your mind as needing something.

Project an image of you embracing the person, or see angels surrounding and protecting them, or if they have financial worries, vividly imagine them paying all their bills on time easily and happily with a triumphant fist punched into the air in victory.

These uplifting visions and thoughts allow the person to find solutions to his own problems. This is their divine purpose. Do not take it from them. Your worry energy only clouds their minds and weighs heavily upon their shoulders.

We often see green soul vibrations spend their entire lives taking care of others. They forget their own needs believing it is their duty to be of service to others. They sincerely want to make people comfortable and happy. They may fuss over them, offering food and drink, and maybe even allow them to borrow some of their own hard-earned money.

It takes an old soul to know how to balance giving with receiving.

Within each of the above scenarios lies the golden opportunity for the soul's advancement by choosing to see beyond the physical and allow its involvement in the physical world to be awakened to the bigger picture of their game board.

Only God can know what is best for each soul. Only God can see all lifetimes and the loose strings that need to be woven into the next life story.

All the moves your soul makes on your game board bring you great wisdom. You are always a winner at the Game of Life.

The Anger Game

Anger is an explosive reaction to an event or confrontation expressed through violent words or even violent actions. Many people today seem to resort to anger as a means of manipulation and control over others. They believe if they can outshout you, they win. These people are emotionally immature. Their insecurity centers around the fear that their needs will not be met. Men are more inclined to use this technique to control others than are women. Mental abuse is only too prevalent in relationships with anger as the game changer.

On the other hand, when anger arises within you like a volcano ready to erupt, it is offering you the opportunity to stand up for yourself against the games people play. **Anger is pushing you to do something to take care of your personal needs.** Act in the moment before the anger boils over. Act while you are still in a calm and peaceful place to speak without allowing your own anger to spew molten lava all over everyone.

These volcanic eruptions occur when people push their anger down into their solar plexus, believing that it is not worth the confrontation it might create. In other words, they do not believe they are worth standing up for! Or they believe the other person is not worth the energy it would take to speak up. By not standing up to a bully who uses anger to manipulate and control you, you are doing a disservice to yourself and the person.

Unfortunately, when your own anger has fueled your emotional engine to overflow like a volcanic eruption, suddenly and without warning, your volcano erupts and everyone wonders what happened because the outburst is out of proportion to the cause that has built over time.

Justice is never served without calm reason and the intent for the good for all involved.

Your spirit cringes from negative, angry words or actions. It fills your body with adrenalin to create that fight or flight urge. Listen to your spirit's emotional gas gauge. If your first reaction does not stop the negative force against you and you find someone "yelling" at you, you might hold up your hand in a "Stop" sign and say calmly, "Would you please repeat that so my ears can hear it and not my gut?" Learn to say, "No. I do not accept that! Let's brainstorm for new ideas to create a win-win situation here." Practice in front of a mirror at finding the words to stand up to anyone who is verbally or emotionally abusive. Become aware when they are trying to manipulate you to take care of their own personal needs. Also become aware when a confrontation may lead to violence. Do not confront. Make plans to leave.

"Liar! Liar! Pants on Fire!"

There are two kinds of games using lies: white lies and black lies. **White lies** are words of false flattery when someone seeks to obtain something from you. Your inner warning system may say, "Oh, oh. What does he want?"

A black lie refers to a deliberate falsehood to manipulate or control another for one's selfish needs. People may lie and cheat to obtain their goals and do not care how it may harm another. Very immature souls find lies have become such a normal way of life, they cannot discern the difference between truth and falsehood.

When confronted with people who lie, your inner warning system awakens. In your world with so much fabrications and outright lies, organizations have formed for fact checking. It is sad that lying has brought humans to this awareness. And yet, we say to you, dear souls, it is a time of great awakening for your species. We have said many years previously that when you awaken to the transparency in politics, you will begin to raise the consciousness of the masses.

The Money Game

Fear of not having enough money for personal needs can drive a person to manipulate and control others so as to obtain financial security.

This is a tendency for younger souls who believe there is not enough to go around. They will be the first at a bargain sale. They may gain pleasure at lording it over another at their great purchase.

Their belief in lack drives one to "Grab it while you can, or it will be gone." It causes people to panic when the stock market does a nosedive. This was behind the 1930s crash when it caused people to make that "Run on the banks" and even drove people to suicide.

They believed in the concept of the "Haves" and "Have Nots" as the natural order of things. Many now believe that the rich get richer and the poor get poorer because that is exactly what has happened in today's world.

When enough hold an image as truth, they will bring it into reality. A change in consciousness is now lifting minds and hearts to the truth of abundance in that all needs are met for every living soul on the planet—if it is for their greatest good to experience it.

We remind you that baby souls do not become adults overnight. It takes many lifetimes playing on Earth's game board before they find themselves winners more often than losers.

Some have said that money is the root of all evil. It certainly can trigger emotions ranging from terror of poverty to excessive greed. Becoming financially independent can seem to be a losing battle for many now on the planet at this time because of the pandemic and so many people without jobs.

And yet, we say unto you: the soul's story is being fulfilled according to God's design.

Periodically you need to do a "fact check" on your "self-talk." Did you say, "I can't afford that?" If so, change it to, "I'd rather spend my money on other things."

The Sexual Manipulation Game

Sadly, we must address the abuses that lead to sexual trafficking. It is perpetrated by infant and baby souls who are in the very first stages of experiencing the game of life on Earth's stage. Their carnal needs overrule their spirit's development of integrity and compassion for others. They see others only as a means to their carnal, emotional and physical needs.

Sexual needs can create a battleground on a couple's game board. Sadly, it is too often used to manipulate and control.

The young soul of the male species equate sex as a physical exercise allowing for pleasure and release of tension. As we have said earlier, baby souls in male form cannot see others as themselves, but only as objects of their pleasure or success.

Most women consciously or subconsciously associate sex with love, marriage and children. An innocent girl may become confused when her lover makes love one moment and verbally abuses her the next moment, and after the verbal beating, wants her to again make sexual love to him.

Women are now demanding respect from men to see them as equals rather than objects of their sexual pleasures. It is a rude awakening for the sex trade, which has also been exposed by your media for the entire world to see.

When giving or withholding sex is used as a game play, look for the underlying fear or need that has not been met and suggest discussing it with your partner to find another way to meet one another's needs. Honesty along with an equal amount of concern can mend a shaky relationship.

The Energy Vampire Game

There is always one person on our game board who has a great need to hear their own voice as they talk and talk and talk until every drop of energy is drained from you. How do they know when there is nothing left? How do we stop them before they steal your last drop our God-given energy?

These souls greatly need someone to really hear and see them. They need validation for their existence. They are starved for compliments and for unconditional love.

If this kind of soul enters your life, it is an opportunity for you to exercise your listening skills as well as your compassion for another in great need of your light. And yet it is an opportunity for you to take care of your own needs. When you are feeling the energy drain from you, stand and walk them to the door…or walk away. Wish them a good evening and thank them for coming.

You have the duty to honor your spirit's needs and say when enough is enough. While it may seem to be unkind or lacking compassion, you have a duty to your own needs. You have a right to end the conversation as quickly and kindly as you are inspired to do in the moment.

As we end this chapter, we would leave you with a new awareness: the games people play on your life's game-board lead to the gift of awareness, which leads to wisdom. As you awaken your inner senses through prayer and meditation and develop your ability to see with inner sight, you know—without knowing how you know—when a person needs your attention and compassion. You hear the voice of your soul and angels within your mind and you learn to play life's games brilliantly in becoming the winner over every challenger including yourself. This, indeed, is the straight path to enlightenment.

We encourage you to practice genuinely finding nice things to say to another. Praise can uplift and support all the players on your game board.

Genuine praise is a wonderful way to raise consciousness for yourself and for the other players in your life's story.

Praise is a gift of the heart. Use it in abundance.

Chapter 14
How Do I Hear
My Guardian Angel?

Most often your guardian angel does not speak to you in words but rather in thought forms, or ideas given telepathically. Because most people are left-brain dominant, they expect words and often miss the messages.

We have presented methods throughout this book in helping you awaken your inner senses that allow you to receive those hidden messages from your guides and angels.

As an archangel, you also have our help whenever you call upon us. Although there are many more of us than the most well-known such as Archangel Michael, Archangel Uriel, Archangel Gabriel and many others. We do not need to supply their names. Simply call upon any of us and we shall always be there to uplift, inspire and encourage you.

Please remember—we are not allowed to intercede to "save" you from yourself. We can only answer when you call upon us.

Also remember that you have a guardian angel who was assigned to you the moment God breathed your soul into existence eons ago. Although you may be new at incarnating within a physical dimension, your soul is ancient. We speak of "soul age" only as it refers to your experience within the physical dimension.

Experience is the key word. When you begin your exploration of a physical dimension, you are like an infant with new senses and physical experiences to help you grow in knowledge of the consequences of your actions and choices **while within your slower-vibrating dimension.**

Again we point out how there is never any judgement of your experiences within a physical dimension. The Creator knows it is only another opportunity for your soul to gain knowledge in how to become a co-creator with Itself.

While in the physical world, your dense energy and your limited awareness block you from being in tune with angels.

We suggest a list of steps to allow you to hear your angel's inner voice:

1. Find a space in your home where you can go to meditate. Bring in candles and icons of your symbols for avatars who guide you—including angel pictures or

statues. You are a physical being. You need physical visuals.

2. After you have removed any clutter from this room, cleanse it with sage to clear any previously negative energy left behind.

3. Sit upon your bed or in a comfortable chair with a small TV tray and your scientific journal where you can write down your thoughts, questions, and inspirations. This will help you set the tone for what you wish to accomplish through meditation.

4. Close your eyes and ask for us to come to you.

5. Breathe slowly, deeply and each time you exhale, imagine all negative energy evaporating from you.

6. Continue to do deep relaxation, concentrating on any part of your body that feels tense.

7. Relax, breathe and wait...

8. When ideas come, quickly write them down.

We are here to serve your adventures into physical worlds as well as anything you do to gain the wisdom you seek.

We once gave Rae a vision during her first experience in group meditation that has stayed with her ever since. We showed her the Master Jesus approaching in his physical form. He held a large black velvet pillow about three feet in dimension. Upon the pillow was a three-foot faceted diamond glowing with light from within it. The Master explained that she was seeing how each person looks out of one of those brilliantly lighted windows upon their world and yet the diamond is God holding within Itself all that is.

We suggest you ponder upon this exquisite vision and feel the peace of God descend upon you and wrap you in the glory of perfect love that is the Creator.

Be prepared for additional visions that will uplift and inspire you. Remember to relax, trust and believe it is not only possible but essential that you contact and converse with your own guardian angel.

Chapter 15
How Do I Unlock
The Power of My Imagination?

Since you and your soul are designed to be co-creators with God, it is your task as a sentient being to learn to supply all your physical, emotional, intellectual and spiritual needs.

Your imagination is the key to unlock the door to manifesting every desire.

In your beginning experiences, it may seem that you fail miserably. We say unto you: **you never fail**. Every action gains your soul new knowledge in what will work and what will not as you strive toward a desired goal. After your soul assimilates the wisdom of such experiments, your soul does not need to repeat it and you advance.

Yet some souls stubbornly go on to try an idea in the same way over and over until they give in to our inspiration to try another way which will lead to the desired goal.

Success builds upon success. If you look back and focus on your failures with a sense that you cannot succeed, you slow your progress of soul growth and continue to experience failure. Therefore, we encourage you to always focus upon your successes and build upon them to gain the confidence that will surge you forward to create whatever you desire.

Whatever you focus upon will become your reality.

It behooves you to become aware of your thoughts to discover your self-talk and to learn precisely what it is you do focus upon.

We have included a fanciful list of the ingredients for a successful, happy life. Add your own grain of salt with the special ingredients known only to you. Unlock your imagination and use this imagery to help you be God's apprentice creator.

Imagine A Formula for Success

Focus now upon awakening your child-like playful imagination as we use the analogy of cooking up a formula for your "Soup of Success." Knowing that you are not a beginner soul, we know **you already have all the ingredients**. Although all sentient beings struggle to communicate with the faster vibrating realms where you find ideas and inspirations, only through experience can you gain the tools needed to consciously add the insights and wisdom of angels to your Soup of Success.

The angels and archangels are here to uplift, encourage, and inspire your soul's success. As you return each time in a physical suit, your spirit's intuitive abilities increase, and your miss-creations decrease. You wake up sooner rather than later—but we know you will never be fully awake until you shed your physical body and return to the realm of your spirit.

Meanwhile, you are here, and when experiencing success, you experience the joy of living. You learn to tolerate the glitches that seem to intrude on your plans. You know that eventually you **will** succeed.

The Recipe for Your Soup of Success

First Ingredient: A fresh new idea seeking to become a physical reality.

When a new idea is given and it causes excitement, it is time for it to become a reality in your life. Your soul is always seeking to use its creative powers to gain new knowledge as a co-creator with God.

Second Ingredient: A positive emotional response.

Whenever an idea enters your mind from the mind of God, it creates an emotional response. It if says "I don't have time for that," then, like smoke, your soul sees a glorious idea evaporate. When you receive an idea and your heart quickens with excitement, you will put your mind and heart and soul into its creation. It becomes a glorious new recipe to share with others as you cooperate in being a co-chef with God.

Third Ingredient: A Playful Imagination

By using your playful imagination, you can advance more readily in bringing forth an idea into your physical reality. Being playful means letting go of the constant need to judge an idea or to label it. Your imagination is merely the ability to image within your mind what success might look like. Using your mind to try out ideas before you put them into action can save you time in wasted trials and errors.

Still, always try out any new ideas as they come to you. You have proven this important ingredient of time and experience and now have the wisdom to know success may not come immediately. Draw on those previous experiences to drum up your courage to **stir the pot and create success!**

Fourth Ingredient: Reel in each new inspiration as it is given.

Study it and ask for clarification or more information. This means time in meditation to receive the responses—for most often, it is not given in words but in additional ideas.

Fifth Ingredient: Become aware of your experienced inner chefs: God and your soul.

You have a wealth of knowledge from God. When you ask, divine inspiration is given. When you ask your soul, past-life experiences may be revealed. Ask to reveal to you all knowledge in relation to your new idea. Perhaps someone who is working with you on your new recipe is feeling conflicting emotions that may be causing unexplained irritation or frustration and is turning your soup sour. Be open to the energy flowing around you and your idea. Release and let go of anything uncomfortable.

Sixth Ingredient: Ask for help from others when it is needed.

But beware of those who would try to take over and do it their way. This is your unique recipe, not theirs. Be firm in their role as assistant chef and refuse help when it feels uncomfortable for you. Also refuse to feel lesser than your helper who flaunts its wisdom, experience or anything as superior to yours. This is your idea, your project. Claim it!

Seventh Ingredient: (The most important element of your Success Soup.)

Create a strong determination to persist in following each new idea wherever it leads you. See failure as only an ingredient that did not work.

There are always some false starts and wrong turns in the process of reaching your goal. **Do not give up!**

God lives and breathes within all created things within your physical world, even with all inanimate objects. Thus all things are expanding and recreating continual awareness from the Creator Itself.

The Condensed Recipe for the Soup of Success

One pound of a fresh new idea from God.

A cup of a positive emotional response

An ounce of imagination

Two cups of new inspirations

One cup of ideas from your Master Chef and your soul

A pinch of outside opinions

A pound of determination for achieving success.

The Gift of Visualizing

So many people have declared they do not know how to visualize. The misperception is wide and varied. Some expect pictures to form when they close their eyes.

In my metaphysical classes, one lady claimed she had taken a course in visualization and had failed miserably. And yet when I suggested she think of a tree, she paused and then said, "Okay..."

I asked her to describe it and the woman said it was big with leaves.

Then, I had her see the tree in winter with snow on the branches. The woman closed her eyes and simply nodded. Then, I was inspired to have her image a red cardinal upon the snowy branch. Again the woman nodded and smiled.

When I congratulated her, saying she now knew how to visualize, her surprised response was, "Is that all there is to it?"

We delighted in the radiance of this woman's lights as her spirit opened to a whole new avenue of communication with her angels and guides. She would bring forth whatever she could imagine and hold it fast within the emotion of joy. And she would share her knowledge with many others when she was inspired to start her own meditation group.

Emotions play a dominant role in each Life

To speed you along your path to enlightenment, we need to speak further about your emotions. Reining in those runaway negative emotions is a giant step forward. First, you must become aware of your dominant emotional state—the emotion you use most often. If you find it to be one of the heavier, darker emotions, then you can strive to pull yourself up until you are experiencing joyous feelings more and more often.

We suggest you pay close attention to the words you use that express your feelings. Become aware of the different energy within your body when you express positive emotions as compared to when you experience negative emotions. Pay attention to the words that express emotions as the statement such as "I feel..." or "I believe..." or "I hate it when..." or "I love it when..."

Only until you become aware of your emotional statements can you and your soul step upon your spirit's conveyor belt to smoothly carry you along on the path to enlightenment.

Detach from the Expectations of Others

We encourage you to bring forth your playful spirit to imagine sitting in the audience and watching yourself on Earth's stage. Use your spirit's imagination and carefully explore the possible consequences of each choice you made this day. Spin out the scenarios to watch how the other characters responded. How did you respond emotionally? What fears have you ignited? What joys?

Some may call this an examination of conscience. See it as a review through your previous emotional reactions in search of gems of wisdom. Do not use this as a means of judging your actions but rather as a review of how your emotions roll through your every waking moment. You are mining emotional gold when you become aware of the negative triggers that cause your discomfort.

Emotional fears and anxieties create stress which is the number one cause of illness. Eliminate as many negative emotions as possible and your health will improve, your life will brighten, and your accounting of good things happening will grow each day.

What you focus upon will become your future reality.

You are always playing a role within the story written by your soul. While your soul is the author, credit is given to those on your Council who help you edit and rewrite for better clarity. The Council's advice may come in an inspirational book such as this one. It may come from a friend or even a stranger. It can come from a friendly smile.

So, although your soul is the writer and director of your story, you are the leading star. There are behind-the-scenes producers, directors and advisors of more experienced souls who help you win that Oscar Award. Give thanks daily for their help. Constantly give praise and grateful thanks to God and all your unseen guides and angels.

We say unto you: "An attitude of gratitude is worth your weight in gold."

When you focus on what it is you desire to make real in your world with a joy-filled heart knowing your desire is already a reality, you speed the messages and ideas that will lead you to your goal. Joy fills your emotional energy tank to overflowing and suddenly there is movement toward your goal.

Each physical life story gains your soul great wisdom. But as we have said previously you cannot transform a baby soul into an adult in one lifetime. **Be patient with self and with others.**

Your Imagination Vocabulary

To build your Imagination Vocabulary, begin using colorful adjectives to describe what you **imagine you see, what you sense, what you smell, and touch, etc.** The more words you use to verbalize the imagery, the more tools you give to your angels and guides to use to send you answers to future questions. They use imagery most often—not words whispered in your ear.

This is a great time to keep adding to your image word dictionary. For example, under S of your alphabetized tabs you may make a list of Sight Words such as bright, dull, dark, shiny, colorful, etc. And under Sound, write the words loud, soft, thundering, gentle, angelic, etc. Under Touch, write the words soft, rough, thick, thin, smooth, etc. Continue with the other inner senses of smell and taste. If you are familiar with using a computer, you can type a word, highlight it, right click and then click on Synonyms to add a whole lot more words.

"Why should I do this?" you may ask. It is because later when you begin to decode your visualizations, we will present **descriptive words to give you an insightful meaning to help you interpret your imagery.**

Once, when I was teaching my eighth-grade English students, I could not get their rowdy behavior to settle down. When I realized anger was about to take over my usual calm demeanor, I turned my back to them (not a smart thing to do!) and took deep abdominal breaths. When I turned around I noticed the room had grown silent.

A boy asked, "What did you do?"

I was puzzled and asked, "Do what?"

"Just then, you...uh...changed."

Ah! I smiled and thought how they must have actually felt my energy changing from anger into inner peace.

I said, "I was angry with all of you for not settling down when I asked."

"But you're not angry now. Why?" The young boy's inner senses were vibrating awake.

The question stumped me. How could I teach a group of teenagers a meditation technique without getting into trouble with the principal? I took another slow, deep breath and asked for divine guidance. Raphael immediately revealed how I could do it.

I first taught my students how to relax and use abdominal breathing, explaining that I had also taught vocal music using correct breathing that allowed a person to sing properly. I added how proper breathing also allowed them to awaken their imagination. Then I said, "Now we'll do a creative writing exercise that will be fun."

"Fun" was my key word in teaching. I always had the motto, "If it isn't fun, I don't want to do it!"

So, we started there inspiring Rae to share with her students the difference between shallow breathing that tightened the body and stole oxygen from the brain versus abdominal breathing that allowed them to relax and calm the body. She listened to our caution not to tell them these were the first steps in meditation.

Then, we inspired her to allow them to practice quiet breathing with their eyes closed while she asked them to imagine a journey through beautiful woods where they meet a small animal. When she could see they were all quiet, she told them to open their eyes and write down as many adjectives as they could to describe their animal.

Next, we inspired her to tell them to imagine the animal as a cartoon character and then write down what it might do or say to them. We suggested she even tell them to draw a picture of it if they liked. This allowed her right-brain-dominant students to find a way to express their vision when words could not do it.

When they were done and allowed to share their experience, the students grew excited and one boy asked, "Can we do this meditation thing again?"

Rae quickly hushed him and said, "It was a creative writing exercise." She was not about to have the principal come knocking on her door.

After this joyously spontaneous experience with her students, we encouraged Rae to repeat the exercise before a test to help her students relax and let go of the tension a test always created. She discovered their scores rose significantly and they asked to do it again before the next test.

To summarize: learn to relax your body through abdominal breathing. Awaken your imagination by visualizing a private place where you find you can relax and be comfortable. Breathe in and imagine as you breathe out, all your tension and anxieties dissipate and are gone.

Continue to breathe abdominally as you relax and allow images and ideas to flow to you. When an idea enters your mind, quickly write it down because like dreams they can quickly disappear.

This, indeed, dear ones, is how you communicate with us. Do it daily more than once a day, as often as you are inspired to do so.

Soon you will find divine inspiration slips in when you least expect it. Lost your keys? Sit down, relax the body, breathe deeply and ask the angels to help you see those keys. You may be amazed at the results.

Chapter 16
How Do I Create
A Happy Home?

Create order and cleanliness within your dwelling place, and your mind and spirit will rejoice.

Again, we refer to negative energy as the basic cause of all dysfunctional beings. When you become more aware of the energy flow within you and within your living space, you will begin to feel better as you take steps to move more often within the flow of positive, happy energy.

This applies even to non-physical things such as your living space. We suggest you study the ancient wisdom of Feng Shui, which is the Chinese understanding of energy called Chi as it flows throughout one's home. While the study can become quite complex, the simple version is to allow pure love energy to flow unheeded around and through all objects within your home. The arrangement of furniture can also enhance and direct the flow of energy by having it arranged more in an oval or circle rather than squared. The idea is that corners can trap negative energy.

It is suggested that since mirrors reflect light, they can also bring more positive energy into the home. Wind chimes create uplifting energy through sound. Fresh flowers or those made of natural products such as silk are preferred over artificial. The arrangement of small objects such as knick-knacks can enhance when used sparingly. When they become a dominating factor and create clutter, they hold the energy and prevent movement.

I read about a man who had a fast-growing cancer. His angels encouraged him to call in a "Feng Shui Doctor" to come to his home to see if anything in it was toxic. Upon entering the house, the Energy Doctor saw immediately what the problem was. Everything was green: green walls, green carpeting and mostly green furniture.

Green signifies growth. This man had unwanted growths in his body. To solve the problem, he was moved out of his house while the walls were painted a soft yellow, the furniture was covered in white, and the entire space was rearranged to flow in circles rather than squares. Mirrors were hung to reflect the good energy. The energy doctor put up wind chimes, brought in flowering plants, set up a small waterfall, placed clear quartz crystals as ornaments in open spaces, uncluttered the clutter including too many knick-knacks and cleaned up the energy through various other techniques, thus creating "Good Chi."

With the good chi now circulating within this man's home, he was slowly healed of cancer.

Most people do not understand subtle energy and how impactful it is upon your health.

Raphael encouraged me to study energy that led to the healing method called "Emotional Freedom Technique" and "Body Talk." I learned how to use kinesiology, which is the testing of the deltoid muscle to allow the body to respond to simple yes or no answers. Energy studies found the body did not lie when asked if a certain object was good for it. For example, if you held a cigarette in one hand and someone tested the strength of your arm by slightly pushing down on it when held outright, the arm would drop. But if you held an apple, the outstretched arm would hold fast as a truth told through the strength or weakness of the deltoid muscle. It worked well and I became good at helping people. Although I became a certified practitioner, I gave it up after realizing how people fall right back into the same emotional energy patterns that caused their illness to begin with.

For example, a woman in my neighborhood reluctantly came to me for help...reluctant because she knew I was an "intuitive" and had mixed feelings about that. Her husband encouraged her to give it a try. Her pain had so debilitated her she could hardly walk and had never been able to have a restful night's sleep.

Being an intuitive, I immediately sensed the woman's energy blockage was due to an emotional tie to a person close to her. After probing a little, I found I was right. I then used the affirmation, "Although I have a sense of loss of my loved one..." while I had the woman imitate where she should tap on the meridians of her own body. Fear, anxiety and other emotional energies block the meridians like a blocked artery can lead to a heart attack.

After the first few tapings the woman reported her pain had lessened but Rae continued repeating the affirmation with the woman mimicking the tapping on the places on her own body's meridians. She worked for an hour having the woman repeat the affirmations until she was able to say her pain was finally at a zero level. The woman cautiously stood, took a step and with eyes wide declared she was "cured."

Rae cautioned her to continue to use the affirmations about releasing her son into God's hands and letting go of her anxieties and fears for his safety. She learned that the mother had not heard from him since he'd stormed out of the house over a year before.

But...she couldn't let go. She was the "chronic-worrier mom," and after having a wonderful pain-free evening and the first restful night's sleep in a year, she reported her pain had returned a few days later. I was so disappointed. Although I continued in this form of healing, I eventually gave up the practice when I saw how often people fell right back into their old negative worry habits.

How to Cleanse Your Home of Negative Energy

One simple way to change the energy within your home is to bless a small portion of sea salt by saying a prayer over it such as, "I ask God to bless this sea salt to cleanse the energy of this home, to remove any negative thoughts trapped here, to raise my consciousness out of fear, doubt, anxiety and any belief in lack so that my home may radiate love, peace and harmony."

Then, go into each room and sprinkle a few grains of that blessed salt in each corner while saying the above prayer. Remember, it is your <u>intent</u> that creates the reality. Remember also that you are a co-creator with God and as you command, so it shall be.

Of course, the first step to cleanse your home would be to clean it and remove the clutter. If you have young people in the home, it would be wise to sit them down and explain the purpose of this ceremony—to bring joy and peace to the home.

We remind you also that if there is unrest and friction between people within the home, it is like shedding a dandruff of negative energy leaving its discord everywhere.

And yet, we say unto you, this simple ceremony of using a physical symbol of peace to cleanse the home can be helpful. You might call upon us to stand guard within each room to protect the space from negative energy deposits.

Do not equate negative energy with negative entities. Yes, there are negative spirits who may try to influence your living space and you. Spirits can and do haunt physical space, but this is not usually the case. It is more often the residue of a left-over argument that becomes your boogie man. Call upon us to cleanse the area quickly and efficiently.

The Native Americans used sage to cleanse their homes, and because of their constant awareness of their spirituality, most lived happy lives. And yet, we remind you that in all races, the human condition brings souls of varying experience and stages of advancement. A baby soul can create havoc anywhere.

In using sage as an energy cleanser, be cautious with fire. The purpose is to light the sage and allow only the smoke to become the cleanser. Douse it with water when you are finished.

We say unto you: it is the symbolism of the act rather than the act. It is your intent that transforms the movement of energy from negative to positive.

Especially in your place of meditation use that pinch of salt as you bless your space and with strong intent to cleanse it of any negative energy. Always call upon us to help in this endeavor.

Use blessed crystals to enhance your space.

The use of crystals can be most beneficial in bringing in strong positive energy. We suggest obtaining three basic crystals: clear quartz; rose quartz and amethyst. The clear quartz crystal brings clarity while rose quartz enhances love energy and amethyst increases your spirit consciousness.

Many people find these stones in jewelry and wear them when they need a boost of energy or need clarity in decision-making.

How to cleanse your Crystals

Periodically cleanse any crystals because they do attract and hold negative energy. Place them overnight in a glass bowl (not crystal but do not put selenite in water) and cover them with water mixed with sea salt. You may also place them outside in the sun and through the night. Blessing them under the full moon can fully charge them as well.

When there is disharmony in the workplace, we have often suggested a seeker bring a clear quartz crystal and place it on a high shelf with the points facing outward. It can absorb any negative energy and bring peace to your space. We suggest you do not allow others to handle the crystal as it will then absorb the person's energy and defeat your purpose.

The Power of Prayer with Intent

Remember always to pray with the purpose of setting your intent for the day, or for a moment when there is disharmony. Remember to breathe deeply into the abdomen without raising your shoulders so that you can cleanse your body of any negative energy surrounding you.

We emphasize, dear one, that you are a powerful energy being. You swim in a sea of energy that is positive, negative, and neutral. Become aware of which is which and choose to transmute any uncomfortable energy into loving, healing energy for yourself and for all those who enter your Earth's stage.

Chapter 17
What About Different Forms of Divination?

Divination is a method of obtaining the answer to a question by seeking help through spirit guides, angels, mystics, channels and many other mystical practices. While we will discuss many forms of divination, we will not recommend any of the many books written on the topics. We encourage you to seek your own angel's guidance in the matter. It will be far more appropriate for you. Although we do make an exception for our "Open-Eye Meditations" where we will supply a basic explanation of numerology and symbology. We recommend that whenever you use any form of divination to receive guidance in decision-making, you first use a form of meditation to lower your anxiety level so as to hear God's divine guidance.

Astrology

Why was I given my particular star sign?

When God created your soul, it infused it with Its own divine energy and sprinkled it with star dust. Then, the Creator birthed you through one of Its seven vibrating rays, setting your purpose and intent and your specific way of experiencing life. Your unique star sign brings you energetic gifts. Your planet's polarities guarantee challenges to keep your life's drama interesting.

You are born under a different star sign for each life, and even after twelve lives, you will choose a different star's energy for the next lifetime.

Each of you brings forth a set of beliefs from your previous lifetime. With each life upon your planet, you have often experienced that Fight or Flight emotion. Some experiences have left scars on your soul that will reappear until you release and heal them. Phobias that have no reason related to a tragic experience in the present life, may be a carryover from a previous lifetime. They likely result from a death such as drowning or dying from a fall off a cliff.

Indeed, we suggest you study astrology to discover both your gifts and challenges. The stars mix with all the positive and negative energy flowing around and through you daily. God has given your life's purposes and the gifts and knowledge to achieve them. The stars constantly emit energy much like your phone number connects only to you.

Although we do not suggest you read your daily horoscope because it has far too broad an interpretation to be totally valid, we strongly suggest you study both the negative and positive pulls from your star energy each moment of your life. With the help of a trained astrologer, you can gain great knowledge from an interpretation of your life's story.

I like to refer to the story of "Sleeping Beauty" as an example of how our lives have what some call a destiny. When it was time for the celebration of the princess' christening, her parents invited many good fairies to attend the celebration. They refused to invite one negative fairy but that bad fairy came anyway and declared the princess would die at an early age from a prick on her finger.

The frantic parents sought to eliminate all spinning wheels from the palace, but, alas, the princess discovered one and her fate was sealed—or was it?

The good fairy contradicted the curse and declared the princess would not die but rather would sleep for a hundred years and then she would be awakened by the kiss of a prince.

I like to view this story as an analogy of reincarnation. It is not a bad fairy who sets up the possible time of your death or as I call it, your "Exit off the highway of life." You may sleep for a hundred years within the bosom of God before you venture back to Earth's stage so your soul can tell a new story.

Your Council of Elders can be likened to your good fairies. They help your soul write your story—without any bad fairies' present. They help you select your parents and the precise DNA for your physical attributes. They calculate the movement of the stars and their planetary positions to set the exact moment of your birth. You are then born with the perfect package of energy for your soul's new body and spirit.

There are bad fairies, if we may continue the analogy, who live within the negative polarity of our planet. They project thoughts and ideas arising from your fears and beliefs in lack or of not being good enough, or of making mistakes, or of looking like a fool.

We send you a mix of other souls to come and go upon your Earth's stage in order to play a part in your story throughout the incarnation.

We will say again and again—you are divine energy—you carry God's essence in physical form. Rejoice in this. Give daily thanks that this is so.

We caution you: **do not obsess over your astrological sign.** Star energy is a gift given by God as It gently touches you through the planet's configurations within your energetic makeup. Your challenges help you face and eventually release fears as you come to love your divine self. Judge not, dear ones. God perfectly designed you to be what only you can be.

God created all things physical within every galaxy or universe and within all non-physical dimensions.

We are not here to explore the mysteries of the universe, dear one. We have come to inform you of your soul and how you began, how you create your world and how you can learn to be happy.

The human species began as a spark of light quickened within the mind of God to separate Itself from Itself. It created your soul who created your physical vehicle of expression so as to have continual communication through your spirit and your brain that receives divine inspiration to express new ideas. It created your intellect to reason and figure out how to bring forth those ideas into a physical reality. It added a dose of emotions to stir your passion to overcome fear and push forward until you succeed.

Your amazing emotions fill with joy as you observe your planet's beauty. Your soul, mind, and spirit store all your accumulated knowledge from exploring your planet of dualities.

Most importantly, God created your soul to absorb the knowledge for Itself. You are much like God's video cameras with your eyes and ears viewing each second of your life. You cannot hide from God. You are created with an ingenious engineering of flesh, bone and blood. God then created a transmitter within you giving It constant communication with you. You call this your brain and intellect. We call it your soul and spirit. The former will disintegrate and die with your human flesh while your soul and spirit will carry all you have learned into the next world and indeed into your next incarnation.

Although we understand this answer may disappoint those who look for new knowledge about their physical world, we have come to bring you new knowledge about your soul and why you are here in the first place.

Be at peace, beloved soul, for God has made you as an extension of Itself to explore the polarities within your planet that force you to experience all the elements of your wide range of emotions that you will label as good or bad, happy or sad. Each new experience leads you to discover the golden treasures of God's wisdom.

As you advance in knowledge and wisdom from many lifetimes, you will express only the positive aspects of whichever star sign you and your council have chosen in this life and will choose in future lives.

We say you are spun from God with the energy of stars specifically selected from your galaxy and combined with the particles of your planet Earth to supply you with a package of divine energy for the exploration of your planet. God activated specific star particles at the exact time of your birth to set the plot and purpose for your story. This star energy becomes daily blessings as well as challenges for you. Your Council of Elders has carefully planned your star configuration to add to the energy of your physical body for your successful exploration on your planet. Each time you return it is for a new purpose and, therefore, a new energy package assimilated for your physical, mental, spiritual, and emotional needs.

Your entire universe adds to and blends with your unique pattern of energy. It serves to increase your ability to absorb new knowledge and to overcome any challenges within the life.

We do not intend to bring forth a study of astrology in this work. As you grow in self-knowledge and gain self-acceptance and appreciation for your divinity, your energy glows brighter, and your heart sings with joy.

We say unto you: God designed you to be Its co-creator of beauty and goodness within your physical world. Rejoice and be glad in this knowledge. Know that God carefully and lovingly chose your specific star selection to enhance your story as you explore all the subtle energies of your planet.

Below Rae gives you a simplified summary of the positive and negative aspects of the energy streaming from your star sign. We ask you to study its positive aspects and enlarge upon them. Observe the negative aspects and strive to rise above them. Rae also added the interesting aspect of choice of precious metals with every star sign alternating between silver and gold. Silver represents feminine energy while gold is more masculine. Often, the sign was chosen to balance the male-female energy within the body/spirit connection.

Aries, The Ram, March 21—April 20

Positive Qualities: *pioneering, administrative, competitive, impulsive, eager, courageous, independent, dynamic, usually lives in the present moment, quick thinking. Prefers gold over silver.*

Negative Qualities: *domineering, quick-tempered, sometimes have violent tendencies, intolerant, hasty, arrogant, "me first" attitude, brusque, lack follow-through.*

Taurus, The Bull, April 21—May 20

Positive Qualities: *patient, conservative, domestic, sensual, thorough, stable, dependable, practical, artistic, loyal. Prefers silver over gold.*

Negative Qualities: *self-indulgent, stubborn, slow moving, argumentative, short-tempered, possessive, greedy, or materialistic.*

Gemini, The Twins, May 21—June 21

Positive Qualities: *dual, congenial, curious, adaptable, expressive, quick-witted, literary, inventive, dexterous, clever. Prefers gold over silver.*

Negative Qualities: *changeable, ungrateful, scatterbrained, restless, scheming, lack concentration and follow-through.*

Cancer, The Crab, June 22—July 22

Positive Qualities: *tenacious, intuitive, maternal, domestic, sensitive, retentive, helpful, sympathetic, emotional. Prefers silver over gold.*

Negative Qualities: brooding, touchy, easily hurt, negative, manipulative, or too cautious, can be lazy, selfish, feel sorry for self.

Leo, The Lion, July 23—August 22

Positive Qualities: dramatic, idealistic, proud, ambitious, creative, dignified, romantic, generous, self-assured, optimistic. Prefers gold over silver.

Negative Qualities: vain, status-conscious, childish, overbearing, may fear ridicule, can be self-deprecating, cruel, boastful, pretentious, or autocratic.

Virgo, The Virgin, August 23—September 22

Positive Qualities: industrious, studious, scientific, methodical, discriminating, fact-finding, exacting, clean, humane, perfectionist. Prefers silver over gold.

Negative Qualities: critical, petty, melancholy, self-centered, can fear poverty and disease, picky, pedantic, skeptical, or sloppy.

Libra, The Scales, September 23—October 22

Positive Qualities: cooperative, persuasive, companionable, peace-loving, refined, judicial, artistic, diplomatic, sociable, suave. Prefers gold over silver.

Negative Qualities: fickle, apathetic, love intrigue, seek peace, pout, indecisive, easily deterred.

Scorpio, The Scorpion, October 23—November 21

Positive Qualities: motivated, penetrating, executive, resourceful, determined, scientific, investigative, probing, passionate, aware. Prefers silver over gold.

Negative Qualities: *vengeful, temperamental, secretive, overbearing, violent, sarcastic, suspicious, jealous, intolerant.*

Sagittarius, The Archer, November 22–December 21

Positive Qualities: *straightforward, philosophical, freedom-loving, broad-minded, athletic, generous, optimistic, just, religious, scholarly, enthusiastic. Prefers gold over silver.*

Negative Qualities: *argumentative, talkative, procrastinate, exaggerate, self-indulgent, blunt, impatient, likes to gamble, pushy and hotheaded.*

Capricorn, The Sea-goat, December 22–January 19

Positive Qualities: *cautious, responsible, scrupulous, conventional, businesslike, perfectionist, practical, hardworking, economical, serious, or traditional. Prefers silver over gold.*

Negative Qualities: *egotistic, domineering, unforgiving, fatalistic, mind rule the heart, stubborn, brooding, inhibited, status seeking.*

Aquarius, The Water-bearer, January 20–February 18

Positive Qualities: *independent, inventive, tolerant, individualistic, progressive, artistic, scientific, logical, intellectual, altruistic. Prefers gold over silver.*

Negative Qualities: *unpredictable, temperamental, bored by detail, cold, fixed in opinions, shy, eccentric, radical, impersonal, rebellious.*

Pisces, The Fish, February 19—March 20

Positive Qualities: *compassion, charitable, sympathetic, emotional, sacrificing, intuitive, introspective, musical, artistic. Prefers silver over gold.*

Negative Qualities: *procrastinating, over-talkative, melancholy, pessimistic, emotionally inhibited, timid, impractical, indolent, often feels misunderstood.*

As you study the above characteristics of the energy streaming from your star sign, become aware of your daily choices. Like dreams that appear in the morning's sleepy wakefulness, so, too do inspirations from your angels through your spirit's nightly journeys out of your physical body. In a later chapter, we will delve into dreams in more detail, but for now we suggest you begin recording your daily choices and their consequences. Note specifically which motivating emotions influenced the choice of action. As you become more aware of how your emotions influence your decision-making, you will be amazed at how often you react out of fear, doubt and anxiety rather than inner peace and self-love.

Numerology

Numerology is an understanding of the energy vibration of each number and combinations therein.

We often repeat how everything is God's vibrating energy within physical manifestation. Your planet is ordered by scientific methodology and has given a vibration significance to the basic numbers from one to ten. We have given a universal meaning in the next chapter on Symbols. You may find additional meanings in researching this.

The study of numerology can be a very accurate and enjoyable experience.

Tarot Cards

The ancient wisdom of the Tarot has been handed down for generations. It has proven itself to be a reliable source of divination. And yet, nothing is 100% accurate. The individual interpreting the cards may be a young soul who seeks to influence the reading for their personal benefit. There are many readers now sharing their wisdom on your YouTube. Learn from them, but always keep an open mind that no one is infallible. It has been a blessing that more people are open to such forms of divination as well as the many channelers who are bringing forth the wisdom of sages through a connection with the spirit dimension.

Inspirational Card Decks

Those who have been inspired by God to create beautiful decks of cards that hold affirmations or uplifting thoughts have blessed the world with powerful energy.

Pendulums

Pendulums are made up of a weight on a string or a chain. Often the weight is a crystal or some kind of metal. The objective is to begin by asking the pendulum to show you a "Yes" and then to show you a "No." Your pendulum will swing either left to right and north to south or it will go in a circle clockwise or counterclockwise.

A pendulum cannot answer future questions although people always ask. It is a law of the universe that anything within your future is always flexible and open to change. You create with a mind set in a certain direction. When you unlock that mind-set and open to new ideas, your future also changes.

Before using a pendulum, always begin with a prayer asking for your guides and angels to move your pendulum. And always ask for your highest and greatest good.

Spirit Guides

You often speak about our "guides." Who are they? Are they people we love who have passed?

Your guides are not loved ones who have passed, although they often hover and send you their personal opinions and ideas. Most are not strong enough to be heard by your conscious mind and are, therefore, not much influence.

Spirit guides are old souls who have been trained to help those still in the physical. They learn how to send ideas telepathically in answer to your needs. Everyone is assigned one or more guides as needed throughout your life. They change as your needs change. Some have expertise in one area. For example, when writing, Rae asks for her writer guides and finds words flow more quickly or scenes become more vividly displayed within her mind.

Always ask your guides for clarity when beginning a new project.

Psychics, Clairvoyants and Intuitives

Everyone has psychic gifts. The soul's Council will add to the life's plan to develop them in any particular lifetime. We encourage you to develop your inner senses. It would only make sense to find a way to add more information when you have a decision to make. By developing the inner senses, you have twice the information. The problem lies when people do not trust themselves. Everyone would love to have an angel step forward and point in the right way to turn or the right decision to make.

We never do that, nor do any of the guardian angels or spirit guides who accompany you on your exploration of Earth. If we supplied all the answers, what would you gain? Answers that lead nowhere. Only through your personal experiments with the gaining of wisdom from heir consequences, can you begin to reap the rewards of advancement. People with psychic abilities will always reflect their soul's development. When the person is more interested in acquiring a following or increasing their income, their information might be compromised. But when they give it freely as in those who are giving it through YouTube, they have a greater credibility.

When a reader says, "My guide is saying…" know they are guided by a spirit they trust to give them truth. When they say, "I see…," they are Clairvoyant, meaning they have inner sight. If they say, "I feel…," they are often Clairsentient as they will get an impression within their physical body as to what is the truth. Only by keeping track of the person's "hits and misses" can credibility build. Even then it is said that the best of Intuitives is rarely more than 80% correct.

This in itself can be a stumbling block for Intuitives when they worry about being wrong. They must have the abandonment of a little child, joyously sharing the information they receive without judging it.

Mediums

Mediums are those who have developed their inner gift of sight called Clairvoyance and the sense called Clairsentience.

They can sense or feel or see those who have passed from this world into the world of spirit—as all of you will do eventually. Your spirit self is an exact duplicate of your physical body. When the body no longer serves the soul's story, it sheds it like a worn-out coat and continues on into the next dimension of spirit. And yet, some spirits can easily move between dimensions communicating with those still in the physical world.

In fact, whenever spirits find a medium, they gather in the desire to communicate with loved ones still within physical bodies.

I'm reminded of a television show called, "Ghost Whisperer." In it, a medium is always seeing those who had passed over and were seeking her help in some way.

I'm also seeing Whoopie Goldberg playing the role of a medium to her great surprise and dismay as she played a character in the movie Ghost.

It is simply a natural process for those who have passed to try to communicate with those still in the physical just to let them know they are safe and happy.

When asked by a client, Raphael has brought forth those who have died. Once a client came through us with the assurance that the person's loved one had not committed suicide. It was a great blessing for those left behind. The act of suicide is often more painful for loved ones than for the person ending his/her life.

Another time, a spirit came through me with a loud and powerful response, "What the @#! are you doing with that man?" It was as if the spirit had been waiting a long time to speak those words to her friend.

Those on the other side are looking after you. They love you and want you to be happy.

And you often show me a bleacher full of spirit friends and relatives doing "the wave" by standing waving their arms and then sitting back down.

They are your cheering section.

We say to you dear souls—you are never alone. We are always tending to your every need. Do not believe we have abandoned you. Although your soul's story may lead you into adventures you would rather avoid, we know your soul's intent is to balance all things, including previous lifetimes.

Chapter 18
What About Prayer and Meditation?

You are constantly communicating with God because you are the very essence of God and It knows Itself.

Yet, we say to you: search for God in every way you are inspired to find It's divine energy.

Large monuments have arisen to honor God. Every religion seeks to create a dwelling place in which to worship their idea of God. All images are valid. God's loving energy dwells within each of them.

Prayer and meditation are an essential part of your soul and spirit's life. People often meditate without knowing it. For example, when driving on a well-known route, a person may fall into a light trance state and arrive home much sooner than they expected, but really the same time. They can get inspiration from their soul and angels during that brief time.

This is how you find answers to your questions and how you learn to communicate with God.

This picture of the Sistine Chapel creates a sense of quiet meditation and awe for many. The great artist, Michelangelo, in expressing his visions of God and heaven draws thousands of people to Rome.

When I visited the Chapel, people were packed tightly together as we strained our necks to study the ceiling way overhead. Comments begin as a quiet buzz but grew louder and louder until a voice blasted over the intercom with a sharp "Silenzio!"

*We were reminded that we were in a church. The quiet lasted for a few minutes before the murmurs grew and grew until another blast of "**Silenzio!**" snapped the crowd back to a more reverent hush.*

Is this not how it is when we try to meditate? Our mind grows quiet as we try to still our thoughts until the buzzing of some unbidden scenario grows and grows until once you are aware you snap, "Silenzio," and quiet resumes.

It is not easy to meditate..

It is indeed difficult for the mind to quiet the inner voices of anxiety as you think about confrontations from the past or chores and duties within the coming days.

It has been said that prayer is talking to God while meditation is listening. Yet, many cannot seem to enter that state of relaxed awareness. Like the woman who came to Rae for treatment caused by the loss of her son, letting go of one's surroundings and going within may sometimes feel like it has a strangle-hold over you. But after you learn to enter an altered state of consciousness, it may seem to be just too easy for you to have conversations with God and Its angels.

This was so with Rae. Once she began typing her thoughts into her computer, she entered a light trance state and we were able to send ideas through. At first, she thought it was just her imagination, but soon our words presented a puzzle when she realized our thoughts were not her thoughts.

When this communication began with Rae, she had never heard of channeling and thus, it took us a bit longer to convince her it was not her imagination speaking those new ideas and thoughts but ours.

We are always waiting for the opportunity to communicate with you dear soul. With this book, we will suggest a simple but effective way of entering the Alpha state of mind where you can discover that kingdom of heaven spoken of by the Master Jesus. He admonished you to become as little children who completely trust God and who have a wonderful imagination. Trust plus imagination are the keys to unlock your inner kingdom.

We share with you a method in which you create an Inner Sanctuary where you can connect with your angels. We call it an Open-Eye Meditation.

Inner peace may seem like an impossible state of being in your busy and turbulent world. Your minds never stop and neither do your bodies that carry you from home to work or school or shopping or worship and back home to crash into a chair and blindly watch television or instead you keep going until you fall into bed to sleep.

And so, you do not consider taking the time to meditate.

We offer you an alternative lifestyle that will increase your energy and slow your mind to capture an angel's inspiration and still allow you time to smell the roses. We offer a safe place within your mind to retreat from a hectic moment to regroup, recoup, and then return with vigor and new ideas for solving problems.

We will ask you to read our written words to guide you through a journey into your spirit's world of the abstract through your powerful imagination. Many gems of wisdom can be mined as you allow your angels and guides to awaken hidden fears or blockages keeping you from your inner joy and peace. Without even thinking about a problem, you can find a solution through this simple form of meditation.

Because you will be writing down what you imagine in each of these guided meditations, you will need a notebook and your favorite writing tool, or you may use your computer. If handwritten, we suggest you use a three-ring binder filled with both lined and unlined paper in case you are inspired to draw what you imagine. If you are artistic, you may also want to use colored pencils which in themselves will reveal more wisdom from this experience. This could be even more valuable. As you describe what you see and feel emotionally during each meditation, you will be creating a sense vocabulary that we can use to bring you information in the future.

We suggest you put alphabetized tabs at the back of your notebook to begin your list of descriptive words that will become your Symbol's Dictionary. We will add some of our definitions in the next chapter.

All of our meditations are building a visual and verbal language for you to communicate with us—your angels and guides.

You will learn to speak telepathically through the language of symbols.

Your angels will use this personal dictionary to flash an image or a memory into your mind at a time when you are trying to make an important decision. As you have been reading this book, you may have noticed how we send an idea or a picture of a past incident with Rae to use as an example of the subject matter we were presenting at the moment.

As you read the meditation, you may want to use a piece of blank paper or a five by eight card to hide the words below to keep them from interfering with the thoughts of the present concept.

For example, if you are asked to imagine a bird, write whatever first comes to mind. If you cannot name the bird, describe its physical appearance as well as its personality characteristics. Pretending it is an animated character in a Disney movie will give you gems of wisdom later when you come back to the Beta mind to translate its meaning.

Steps to Enter a Meditative State

There are five simple steps for all our "Open-Eye-Meditations." Briefly they are:

First: *Relax the body.*

Second: *Do deep abdominal breathing.*

Third*: Awaken your imagination to envision a playful version of an object or thing.*

Fourth: *Describe the image using as many descriptive words as possible. These will be invaluable later when you interpret your vision.*

Fifth: *After the meditation, go to the Symbols Interpretation in the next chapter and decode the messages given to you.*

Create Your Inner Sanctuary

*Our meditations require the rather tricky part of taking you to your Alpha state of mind that is the sleep state **and yet we ask you to remain awake**. We encourage you to sit straight upright at a table and keep your eyes open using a notebook to record your ideas and visions, which, as we have said, you will later interpret with amazing insights.*

Avoid any distractions during this time. We suggest you turn off your cell phone and silence any background music. You may close your eyes periodically to better visualize an idea but practice doing it with your eyes open as often as possible as it builds your intuition and more quickly opens those Four Clairs we spoke of earlier.

Find a comfortable chair where you can put your feet solidly on the floor. If your legs are too short, place them on a footstool or on a couple of pillows to bring your knees level with your hips, but keep your feet flat and your back straight. Again, we remind you this is not your usual meditation where you lie down, relax and sometimes fall asleep, although some people may at first doze off because we are taking you close to that sleep state.

We encourage you to pause, breathe and relax giving yourself time for ideas and images to form in your mind *and then take enough time to write down your description of what you see, sense, and even smell or hear.*

People who are right-brain dominant will find these meditations simple and easy. For those of you who may be quite creative but use your mind daily for numbers or other left-brain tasks, you might take a bit more effort to shift into your playful imagination and let go of the facts. Yet, you will be using your left brain to search for words to describe what you visualize. These open-eye meditations will help balance your brain hemispheres and allow for better decision-making in the future.

Avoid trying to interpret what you imagine while you are seeing it as it will take you out of the Alpha state of mind. It is important to stay focused on the ideas without interruption from your factual mind.

And with the last step—the interpretation—we will help you decode the messages given to you.

After experiencing this meditation, we suggest you practice going to Alpha at least once a week until you can go there within a few minutes at any time of the day or night. This simple exercise can make all the difference in your life for it will bring you solutions to problems and inspirations to bring forth all you desire.

Again, we encourage you to keep a log of your experiments. We assure you it is safe to jump into this pool of clear, warm water and learn to swim in the spirit realm. No one will be judging your writing or giving you a grade. Misspelled words or typos are to be ignored because they will jerk you out of the Alpha state of mind and close off any messages from us and your guides and angels. When you make judgments about what you see or sense, you snap back into Beta-consciousness and find yourself Beta-bopping! Beware! It can happen. And if it does, simply breathe deeply (no shoulders rising!) and relax. You are safe. And this exercise is greatly worth the effort.

How to Meditate with Eyes Open

First Step: Relax the Body

By focusing on each step below, you will keep the left hemisphere of the brain occupied. Try not to let your mind wander. Our objective in it all is to stop the babbling mind and allow it to relax so as to open the imagination where all creative ideas originate.

1. Take a slow, deep breath through your nose.

2. Release the breath slowly through your mouth as if blowing the air through a straw. Feel your body relax as you let go of all the day's concerns. This is your time. Enjoy it.

3. Tighten your toes... Then let them relax. Pull your feet up while keeping your heels on the floor... Then relax. Push your feet down... Relax... Breathe.

4. Imagine your feet are glued in place. Try to lift them. Feel the muscles in your legs and thighs tighten. Relax and let go.

5. Take a long, deep breath and release it slowly. Relax... Breathe.

6. Tighten your buttocks muscles... Relax.

7. Tighten your stomach muscles... Relax.

8. Pull your fingers into a fist. Hold it...then relax and stretch your fingers out. Let go and Relax.

9. Drop your hands onto your thighs. Breathe deeply. Imagine your hands are now glued to your thighs. Try to pull them off, but you cannot... let go of all the day's concerns and relax.

10. Move your shoulders up to your ears...Drop your shoulders and relax. Then move your shoulders forward... slowly move them back... Relax.

11. Turn your head slowly to the right... Ease through any discomfort. Breathe deeply and relax.

12. Slowly bring your head back to center. Pause and relax.

13. Slowly turn your head to the left. Ease through any discomfort... Slowly bring it back to center... Relax.

14. Bring your chin gently down to your chest. Move it back to center... Breathe and relax.

15. Lift your chin as high as you can... Move your head back to center... Pause... breathe deeply and relax.

16. Lift your eyebrows... Let them relax.

17. Pucker your mouth. Relax and breathe deeply before reading what is next.

Continue using the blank sheet of paper under each section below as you read the instructions. Any time you find tension in your body, breathe deeply and allow your mind to focus on your playful self-awakening. Keep your shoulders down and relaxed. Breathe deeply whenever you feel your mind wanting to control or analyze emotional reaction to the imaging.

Step Two: Awaken your imagination.

Always accept your <u>first</u> thought as the best. Rethinking causes Beta-bopping!

Visualize the number nine – Draw it on your paper and then imagine it standing beside you like a three-dimensional statue. How tall is it? Pretend that you now have magic powers to create this number-nine statue out of **anything** with the wave of your hand! Swirl your writing hand clockwise over the number until you have an idea of what the number nine statue looks like.

Take your time... breathe... relax...

Write down your impressions, using as many descriptive words as you can. This will give you more information later when you interpret what you have seen.

Leave space below your description of the nine's interpretation you will discover. Do not try to interpret anything now as that may pull you back into the conscious, judgmental Beta mind. Pause now, relax, and breathe. After you have described this statue with as many words as you can, watch it slowly disappear.

Visualize the number eight and draw it on your paper. Now imagine it standing beside you. How tall is it? Close your eyes and see it. What is it made of? Take a deep breath and free your imagination to join in on the fun. Do not try too hard. Allow ideas to pop into your mind. Give yourself time. Relax and let go. Breathe...

Describe what you imagine the number eight looks like. When you have written as many descriptive words as possible, the number eight will slowly disappear.

Visualize the number seven as it appears in front of you. Allow your playful mind to create it as a three-dimensional statue. Examine it. Go up to it and smell it. Touch it. Jot down your impressions.

When you are finished, the number seven will vanish.

Visualize the number six as it materializes before you. Draw the number on your paper. See it clearly as a three-dimensional statue beside you. Breathe deeply and let go of any fear that you cannot do this. Write down what the number six statue looks like. Can you touch it? Describe what it feels like.

When you are finished, the number six will fade away.

Visualize the number five as it stands before you—a three-dimensional statue. Breathe deeply and allow the number five to appear in all its glory. Does it have a color, a texture, a smell? How big is it? Describe it with as many visual and sense words as you can.

When you are finished, the number five will vanish.

Visualize the number four that appears in front of you as a statue. Describe its size, texture, smell, taste. Awaken your five inner senses. Use as many descriptive words as you can.

When you are finished, the number four will evaporate.

Visualize the number three that now appears in front of you. Describe it... Take your time. Relax and let go of any judgmental thoughts of how well you are doing.

When you are finished, the number three will disappear.

Visualize the number two that now stands beside you. Describe it. Take your time to smell, touch, and even taste it—(only if that is comfortable for you). Awaken your inner senses.

When you are finished, the number two will vanish.

Visualize the number one as it rises before you. Describe what first pops into your mind. Your angels and guides are sending you more information.

Relax, breathe deeply and go deeper—
Visualize the number one slowing turning into a door.

- Describe the door with as many words as possible. Which way does it open? On which side of the door is the handle? Describe the handle.

- Open the door. Does it open away from you or toward you? Write this down.

- You are now entering a place in nature filled with bright white light. It has all your favorite trees and flowers. You can create beautiful lawns that never need mowing. Create a source of water... Describe it.

- This perfect place in nature is now your "Inner Sanctuary." Here you are safe and loved beyond measure.

- A shining being of light appears nearby. It welcomes you with open arms. You step into the most wonderfully warm embrace of total unconditional love. Bask in this for a moment. Breathe in this perfect love. It is only for you in this moment in time.

- Breathe in the perfect beauty of this space. Smell the perfume of fresh air. Feel the warmth of sunshine and a perfect sky above. Create a resting place and write a description of it.

Rest in this inner sanctuary for a quiet moment.

You can go to your Inner Sanctuary at any time of the day or night, especially when you feel stressed or sad or out of sorts.

Whenever you choose to return to your Inner Sanctuary, follow the steps above in relaxing the body and lowering the brain waves to the Alpha state—and you will immediately be there.

Each time you return, add anything of beauty or comfort that inspires you.

To return, simply take a few long, deep breaths, and consciously relax your body. Visualize the numbers counting backwards and allow your imagination to take you there to feel the love and compassion and wisdom of your being of light. It is always within you, always ready to bring you wisdom and pure love and acceptance. In this inner sanctuary, you are seen as perfect exactly as you are.

Your brain is now functioning from the mind's right hemisphere that allows you to let go of your labeling and your doubts in order to open your imagination.

Each day spend time in your Inner Sanctuary imagining it more clearly each time until whenever you enter, it brings a smile and an instant sense of inner peace and joy.

If you experience anything less, we suggest you go back to the first preparation of relaxing the body and letting go of the left hemisphere's labeling, judging, or skeptical evaluation. Do not allow your mind to try to interpret what you see. Only afterward can you write a description of your feelings and visions. It is only after you return to the Beta mind, that you can begin the interpretation process.

Do you remember in Rae's classroom situation, where her students noticed that she had changed? It was because she had gone into her Inner Sanctuary and replaced anger with inner peace. Once you master this form of meditation, you can go there anytime, anywhere and in only a few minutes. It is an especially good thing to do when you feel tired or sad or out-of-sorts. This visualization will energize and uplift you. Use it daily.

Step Three: Decode Your Visions

With our help, you are about to gain an amazing amount of knowledge about yourself. We will help you translate what you saw, sensed, felt or knew as you wrote a description of the visions given in this first open-eye meditation. You entered the world of the imagination. Symbolism is the key. Whenever you "decode" your visions, remember to avoid self-judgment or self-blame. That will swing you right back into your awake mind. We hold no judgement for you. Nor does the Creator.

Go back to the number nine to read what you wrote and then go to the next chapter on Symbols to see our brief interpretation of numbers and colors. You will find the interpretation of nine to mean "Endings, transitions..." etc. How you described your number nine was a message from your angels about how you may be emotionally experiencing any endings or transitions in this moment or in the recent past.

If, for example, you saw the number nine as made of cement and described it as rough and hard, then whatever challenge you are experiencing right now is likely rough and hard because the number nine represents transitions, endings, or completions.

Use the symbols dictionary for each of your descriptions of the numbers. Check with the number's meanings and compare them to how you described your number. Most people are surprised at how accurate this is.

Chapter 19
How Do I Interpret the Symbols?

After you have experienced your first guided meditation in a trip into your Inner Sanctuary, you can then begin to enjoy the opening up of your intuition and discern the deeper meanings within your visualizations.

For example, you likely have had the experience of a song coming on the radio that described your emotional level of expression perfectly. We often send you messages like this. Now that you are awakening your inner senses, you will recognize them and rejoice in knowing we are always with you, uplifting you and inspiring you to be happy.

Do not be discouraged if you could not quite imagine everything that was presented in this first visualization. It might take a few times before you can get your conscious mind out of the way. If you are so used to analyzing, judging, categorizing, labeling, and so forth, you may find it hard at first to stop the chatter of your left brain.

This is the reason we encourage you to keep your eyes open, although it can be more difficult for some. This method allows you to use your imagination in your everyday waking life. By learning to relax during times of stress when you need your eyes open, you learn to focus on deep breathing and the door to your playful imagination opens and solutions pour out. Get ready to find some amazing insights as you interpret the visions you will receive.

For now, write your interpretation of this guided visualization without the help of the Symbols interpretation. After you allow your own guides and angels to help you interpret what you saw and felt, then you will want to check out our interpretation of the numbers and colors, etc.. Even then, do not accept these interpretations as absolute truth. If it does not feel right, search for another interpretation.

Remember all interpretations must be seen with unconditional love and non-judgment for yourself and others while within your Inner Sanctuary. Nothing negative is allowed.

It is only natural for the factual part of your Beta mind to want to interpret your visions even before you have finished. Do not allow it to interfere. Focus on staying at the Alpha level of mind and within the right hemisphere. Only then can your angels and guides slip in new information that will uplift and enlighten you toward raising your consciousness.

Too often, people tend to criticize their thoughts and actions in their desire to "grow spiritually." They believe they have to overcome every small imperfection.

This is fallacy. You are perfect right now in this moment in time. Seek first to learn about your gifts and talents and how to use them for your own good and for the good of others.

An Interpretation of Numbers

Quantum Physics says that the Universe can be explained in numerical equations. Studies find that each number vibrates at a specific frequency and is associated with sound and color because like everything that exists, numbers are energy. For example, the number one is associated with the color red and is the slowest frequency of all the numbers. It has a sound close to the vibration of middle C on the piano. It is also associated with new beginnings as in a fresh start.

Below are universal interpretations of numbers and colors and various other symbols found in dreams as well as in everyday life. Native Americans saw all of nature as the Great Spirit speaking to them.

Begin today looking for messages from your angels and guides in the world around you. Avoid looking for negative signs. Use our interpretations to help you understand the gift of symbols.

We suggest you always go within your Inner Sanctuary and ask your guides to help you with the true meaning of any symbol.

As we have said before—everything is vibrating energy. Numbers and colors have their own particular sound waves that we describe in its relation to your life experiences. Since all you sense, hear, touch, smell, see, or taste also has a vibration and a color, think of life as walking through energy rainbows of pleasant electrical impulses that can create an emotional response as well as trigger a visual idea.

Think of people as walking-talking rainbows reflecting the magnificence of God. Appreciate them for the beauty of their divine light.

Numerical Interpretation

Number 1 — Keywords: new beginnings; fresh way of seeing something. The number one vibrates to the energy of new beginnings with new creative ideas or new relationships. It may include new projects or may refer to your individuality. It has to do with initiative which can create restlessness in the need for new experiences. It is a time for making decisions on your own without help from others. Other words to describe the energy of the number one are independence, original thinking, being a pioneer, a leader who is self-reliant, strong-minded, a person who thinks out of the box.

Be playful with the numbers you see in everyday life. Look to them as ideas coming from your guides and angels, knowing they give only positive uplifting messages. Anything negative comes from your own fearful emotional energy.

Number 2 — Keywords are balance and harmony in all situations. Two has to do with the energy of partnerships, business or legal or a love relationship. It has to do with decision making; balance; cooperation; mediation; passivity; patience; decisions or choices to be made between two things. It is a time of seeking peace through arbitration or compromise. This number calls for patience, tolerance and suggests that you not always be too quick to please.

Focus on the number two with harmonious emotions when you need to have a one-on-one conversation in which there may be uncomfortable responses. Focus on seeing or imagining smiles and handshakes as the result. Always use your imagination for positive energy and the results will be positive.

Number 3 — Keywords are creativity, playfulness, imagination. *The number three expresses abstract ideas in a multiple of ways: through verbal or written communication; through art or design or decorating. Number three people are good teachers, sales reps, preachers, etc.*

Three brings creative energy for a new project; for socializing or entertaining; or it may cause a bit of scattered energy. It has the drive for seeking freedom through self-expression. The number three also holds the vibration of happy ideas such as gathering people together for a party. Some say things happen in three's, but if that refers to anything fearful, such as how some people view death, do not allow such a thought to enter your consciousness.

We remind you of the wise old saying, "As you think, so shall it be." You are a student of creation under the Master Creator, God. Your emotions drive a thought or idea into a physical reality. Ground each thought of fearful results that could become your reality. Recognize each thought's basic emotion and choose to use only joyful ones.

Number 4 — *Often refers to a job or career. If you are unhappy in this area, it could be encouraging you to think about a change. It also refers to stability as with four legs of a chair firmly planted on the floor. It can refer to law and order, or any physical form built as a result of a merger or expansion. It always refers to balance. It depends upon what words you used to describe the number four.*

I like to watch the numbers on my digital clock and interpret them as messages from my Raphael. I often add the numbers together for another interpretation. I'm reminded to always associate the numbers only with harmonious thoughts.

Number 5 — Centers on communication. It often deals with decision making. It denotes change, bringing a restless energy that keeps you on the move. It could literally refer to a physical move or change of address. It also could suggest travel. It calls for organized thinking, being practical, being a person who is a hard worker and disciplined. It can refer to the need for communication and emotional freedom. It can express itself as restlessness; being on the move; desiring to travel or seek new knowledge or new intellectual interests.

As an example, once I kept seeing the number 555 on the digital clock at the same time I heard, "Move." I shook my head and ignored it because I was very content right where I was. But the energy kept pushing at me until I finally began looking for another place to live. Each town I visited had nice homes for over $100,000 but they were in very run-down neighborhoods. I kept looking until I came to "Michigan Blvd." I laughed and told my friend to turn left where we found the house I would soon own. But my next problem was that I had no money for a down payment. I heard Raphael say, "Look for a mortgage company." I did and found one who after checking my credit score and my income as a teacher and Social Security decided to carry the mortgage. I was amazed and grateful for my new home on nearly an acre of land amidst woods that reminded me of my home in Michigan. It has been an amazing blessing where I've built a large Labyrinth that I walk nearly daily. And...my only neighbor is a young couple who have adopted me and take care of all the physical things I cannot do. Talk about miracles!

Never accept another's negative interpretation of this number five. For there are always people who look to the downside of everything. You are participating in a world of duality, but what you choose to focus upon will become your reality and will reflect your soul's experiences upon your planet. Older souls will always find good in any negative situation.

Number 6 — *Has to do with the need for harmony, peace, and beauty with emphasis on home and family or partnerships. It may refer to balance in a marriage or improving your ability to listen to another's problems. It may refer to balance and harmony regarding your health or bringing order to your surroundings by eliminating clutter that can reflect mind clutter slowing the ability to make good clear decisions.*

This number can also refer to those who are your support group. Give thanks daily for those souls who have agreed to be a part of your excursion upon your planet.

Number 7 — *Is symbolic of rest and relaxation. It encourages time for meditation and introspection with a self-analysis of achievements, health, and rest—both physical and mental. It speaks to a need for expanding spiritually, a call for quiet and contemplation.*

We encourage you to set time daily for meditation. It is why we have included so many in this book. We use this method to help you see your life as one continuous conversation with God and with those beyond who love and support your journey to Earth

Number 8 — *Can refer to the business world of money as in earning, receiving, owing, investing of financial resources, etc. It can refer to the law of balance, or what is called Karma or the law of cause and effect in what goes out often comes back*

around. It refers to a time to reap what you have sown during the previous eight days, eight months or eight years. Money issues often crop up requiring a need for more responsible spending.

The number eight can refer also to a need for balance in relationships or for a need for self-discipline. Turn this number sideways and you have the symbol for eternity. Meditate on this as well.

Number 9 — *Refers to endings, or completions, or transitions. It can encourage the reviewing of past actions to discover the wisdom within them. It refers to an "examination of conscience a re-evaluation of goals." It looks at how you are giving to others: either too much or not enough. It speaks of being of service.*

The nine also suggests a putting away of self-judgment and embracing the wisdom hidden within every experience. Everything that your soul experiences while in the physical dimension will bring spiritual growth and better decision-making in your future.

Symbolic Meaning of Colors and Metals

Colors, like numbers, are vibrating their unique energy of light and sound. As light splits into different wavelengths and vibrates at different speeds, it can be labeled as color. Colors affect your emotional, physical and mental states without your even knowing it. Colors can reflect your mood or even change your mood. You choose your clothes by their color vibration. Even if you do not know it, your closet could say a whole lot about you.

Remember: the more descriptive words you add to your meditation experiences, the more messages you will gain from your angels and guides.

Colors have powerful energy. Your planet is blessed with vivid colors that can delight and uplift your spirit. Take time to observe a sunset and allow its energy to fill you with inner peace. Observing the colors within your planet can raise your consciousness quickly and speed you on your path to enlightenment.

***Red** energy is grounded in the Earth. It represents bravery, passion, sexuality, sensuality, courage and determination. It can represent anger as in, "He's seeing red!" Or it can represent bravery. "You deserve the 'red badge of courage!'" It is the color of the root Chakra within our physical/spirit bodies.*

***Orange** represents divine energy as well as leadership with a gentle hand. It denotes creativity, wisdom and compassion. It infuses one with ideas for creating something practical but beautiful. It is also the color of the second Chakra.*

***Yellow** represents the intellect as well as the emotions ranging from deep fear to great joy. It stresses one's need to find happiness. It also represents energy and new ideas to create fun. It is the color of the third Chakra.*

***Green** is considered the color of healing, of growth, both physical and spiritual. It represents caring and generosity. It is often referred to as a symbol of money. It is the color of the fourth Chakra also called the heart Chakra as it centers on giving and receiving love.*

Sky Blue centers on communication of ideas through art, written word, spoken word, performance in dance, music, etc. It suggests speaking your truth. It represents a need for peace and harmony. It can refer to feeling blue or sad. It is also the color of the fifth Chakra.

Dark Blue or Indigo refers to expansion of ideas, of harmony and balance, of creative energies, of thinking out of the box. It refers to an inner knowing or sixth sense. It is also the color of the sixth Chakra within the physical/spirit bodies centered on the third eye or intuition.

Violet or Purple refers to spirituality, mysticism, a seeking of the divine, of seeing into other dimensions. It suggests raising one's consciousness into the realms of spirit and joy.

White is often associated with purity. It is also a blending of all the colors by raising one's vibrations out of darkness into the light of joy and wisdom. It is also the color of the eighth Chakra.

Black is the color of mystery or things hidden. It is a blending of all the colors representing balance. It is often used by those who wish to remain in the background—or wish to look thinner. It also represents endings and completion.

Brown refers to being grounded or gathering your energies or wits about you. It means planting one's feet firmly on planet Earth.

Pastels can mean a softening of the vibration or an immature view of an experience. For example, pink is often associated with infant girls, whereas pink roses are associated with love—often a new love or an immature love. In contrast, red represents a more mature love while deep red would represent a passionate love.

Secondary Colors can be interpreted as a combination of the main colors listed above and thus the mixing of the energies.

Silver often is said to be feminine energy. It refers to maintaining balance, to gaining strength to begin another cycle. It is passive, receptive, and open to new ideas. It denotes generosity, nurturing and a desire to be of service to others.

Gold refers to masculine energy and earthly riches. It could refer to the "Midas Touch" or greed. It also refers to strength, courage and boldness to go after personal desires and dreams.

Copper is often used in healing. Some say it affects the neurological and cardiovascular systems within the body as in using copper bracelets to ease the pain of arthritis. Since it is the main ingredient of the penny, it could be interpreted as cheap.

Remember when you are given any symbol, you need to go to your angels and guides and ask them for the interpretation. You, as humans, tend to first interpret symbols with a negative connotation. Angels and guides look deeper.

Stainless Steel is a hard, shiny metal that could be interpreted as strength or a willingness to look at one's self with clarity. It could use the word "stainless" in another connotation of something being sinless or free of stain.

Pewter was a metal used by the pioneers for dinnerware for its unbreakable quality and durability. Now it is considered a precious metal.

For any other colors you may find in your meditations or dreams, look to the emotional energy of the color for a definition. As you see above in describing pewter, look for the use or clichés regarding the color as well as the Chakra meaning for additional interpretations. We are always speaking to you when you begin to observe the subtle energies surrounding you.

Miscellaneous Symbols

__Wood__ is made from trees and suggests solidity, strength, being grounded, etc.

__Vehicles__ represent your physicality, your "vehicle of expression." For example, a truck or van may represent your work life or your responsibility to family, whereas a sleek convertible may represent your recreational life, or your desires for attention, or wealth and affluence.

__People__ who come into your awareness while awake or in dreams may represent a mirror for you to probe deeper into your subconscious. Sometimes people who pop into your mind can be a telepathic call for you to send positive energy to them. Or they could be telling you something about themselves you did not know.

Descriptive Words for Sensory Perceptions

(Add your own adjectives as well)
__Smell:__ sweet, sour, heavy, light, bitter, sharp, suffocating, calming...

__Taste:__ sweet, sour, bitter, pungent, tart, salty, warm, hot, cold...

Touch: *smooth, soft, hard, rough, prickly, bumpy, warm, hot, cold...*

Sound: *hum, clank, ping, musical, loud, soft, thunk, clock-like tick...*

Sight: *picturesque, clear, bright, dark, dim, cloudy...*

Chapter 20
More Guided Mediations

We choose the above picture as an example of how Raphael's guided meditations open up new worlds. I was inspired to create this mosaic after seeing the "Mosaic House" in Midland, Michigan. The "Spiral Angel" was made from a 3' X 5' piece of plywood painted with primer. Then I sketched the angel and began using grout to attach broken dishes to the plywood. I used mirrors as the background. It was like putting together a jigsaw puzzle where you got to cut the pieces to fit. I hadn't realized that I had put in seven spirals until it was all finished. Seven is a very spiritual number.

This kind of creativity is the result of awakening your imagination through guided visualizations. This is why we have included more guided visualizations so as to give you practice in awakening your gift of inner sight.

Let us emphasize the value of any type of meditation. While many guided meditations are good for relaxation, our meditations expand your conscious and superconscious awareness simultaneously. It goes one step further by inviting your angels, guides and soul to help you interpret the messages given to you during a visit to your imaginary inner hideaway. Nothing is specifically dictated to you to imagine. For example, if you are asked to visualize a tree we do not specify the size, type or emotional impact of what you see. What you visualize has a volume of information to give you knowledge and wisdom.

Once you learn the meanings of these symbols, you might try to impose an image upon your imagination because you believe it to be better or more appropriate. For example, we have found people choosing a purple flower believing purple to be more spiritual. We found that the flower shifted to a sunflower, bright yellow and happy. This is proof that your angels are working with you and it is not just your imagination fooling you.

Always prepare for each meditation by using deep abdominal breathing while slowly relaxing each muscle from your toes up your legs to your body and to your shoulders, face and head. This is essential for you to exit the Beta mind and enter the Alpha state for real meditation. Remember if you get a negative response such as a scolding or a criticism, it is not your angels speaking but your self-doubt and self-criticism. It means you have not gone deep enough in your relaxation to enter the Alpha level of mind where images come unbidden and humor is the rule of the day.

Meditation # 1 Cartoon Fun

Tools Needed: Unlined paper, pen, pencil with eraser, and colored pencils, if desired.

Pretend you have been hired by the Walt Disney studios to create a series of number characters that you will animate and bring to life on the movie screen. You are to visualize the following numbers as these animated cartoon characters. Use words to describe each character. Draw it if you wish, but the words are more important as they could have double meaning for you.

Playfully visualize the character of number **Four**. *What colors come to mind for this animated figure? What is the number wearing? Look for color and design. What is it doing? Write down every detail using as many descriptive words as you can.*

Become a child now and see this number with humor and joy as you imagine it speaking to you.

Breathe! Be playful. Have fun!

Visualize the number **Three**. *Describe it. What does it have to say? Breathe and relax as you describe it in a verbal picture with color, touch and texture, and even sound. Does a song come to mind with this number? Be open to spontaneous ideas.*

And now meet your number **Two** *character... Use as many words as your playful imagination can conjure up. Let go of trying to figure out its meaning or purpose in this vision.*

Now the number **One** *character materializes before you. Describe how different it is from all the others. Breathe! Believe! Allow!*

The number one turns into the door that opens to your Inner Sanctuary. Enter and feel the radiance of your special place.

Allow your guide to embrace you with pure love. Feel peace and love surround you.

Ahead of you is a path—describe it. Look at your feet. What are you wearing?

Your guide walks along a path with you to your special dwelling place. You enter and begin to add things of comfort as if you were designing your perfect home. Breathe deeply and observe our amazing tools of Clairvoyance, Clairaudience, Clairsentience and Claircognizance that are like magic wands as you use them to create your perfect place where you can commune with angels and God.

Go and sit in your comfortable chair. (If you don't have one, create it!) Be comfortable as you turn back in this book to the chapter on Emotions.
Turn on your holographic viewer and place your spirit body on the screen. As you observe each emotion listed, watch your body's reaction to the energy as it responds to either positive or negative feelings. Where did you feel it in your physical body? The solar plexus? The heart area? Your temples? Write this down.

Describe the difference between your reactions to positive and negative emotions? Take time to describe this so you can be more acutely aware of your emotional fuel gauge in any future scenario. Breathe deeply and remain still as you go through the list. Write down what you observe.

Observe where you were and with whom when an uncomfortable emotion rose up. Was there a different reaction you could have taken which would have reaped a happier response? Whenever you feel those signals in your body, breathe deeply, relax, imagine yourself in your Inner Sanctuary...and then observe how your body feels. Do you feel the difference? Although you may be in your Beta mind doing this, when you can feel or sense your emotions, you are in the Alpha mind as well.

On your holographic viewer, observe yourself with another person who displayed a negative emotion. Now imagine a different conclusion. See it on your holo viewer. Remember you are the author of your story.
Knowing each moment of your life is a choice, what decisions have you made that caused you to feel uncomfortable, sad, angry, or... shamed? Again, imagine a different choice. How might you then feel?

Study which emotions are most dominant in your life. Determine to raise your consciousness into joy more often. Do you perhaps need an attitude adjustment? Are you more of a pessimist than an optimist? A cynic believes the worst and searches for facts to prove it, while a skeptic will withhold judgment until more facts are available. An optimist will always search for the good in every situation—and will find it. Which are you? Which attitude will bring you more laughter and joy?

Meditation # 2
Numbers Bring Memories

Always begin your meditation with the relaxation exercise along with deep breathing. For easier focus, use a blank sheet of paper to cover the words that you are not yet ready to read. Focus only on the information or vision presented.
We will let Raphael guide you on this inner journey.

Visualize the number **nine.** Since its energy vibration represents endings, resolutions, or transitions in your life, let it bring to you a **memory** of an **unhappy ending** from your past. Take time to feel those negative emotions. Breathe deeply and slowly. When you are ready, continue to the next paragraph.

Observe where you feel the pain of that emotion in your body. Breathe into the discomfort and then imagine you have a large eraser and you are able to release your holographic image of that painful emotion within your spirit body. Erase the unhappy memory and replace it with the divine light of God. Imagine your soul is now healed of that wound.

Imagine the number **eight** revealing memories of anxiety concerning **money**. Recall various situations where the lack of money gave your spirit pain and anxiety. Picture this number eight with these concerns detaching from you and blowing away in a gentle breeze. From now on, you will open your mind to allow prosperity and abundance to replace fear of lack.

Allow the number **seven** to bring memories of **religious experiences** that might have formed some of your fear concepts of God when you were a child. What did you do with those uncomfortable beliefs? How did you resolve your growing and expanding awareness of God? Release anything uncomfortable into the healing light of your Creator.

The number six focuses on home and family. Allow your soul to bring to you any incident, person, or thing regarding a negative experience in relation to your parents, siblings, or significant other that may need releasing into the light. Breathe and relax. Allow visions or ideas to come unbidden.

(Please note: if anything becomes uncomfortable, do not continue. Skip to the next visual.)

The number five vibrates to **sudden changes** in your life. Recall a change you fought because you did not like it... but it came anyway. Can you now see the good that came from that change? Release any anxiety, fear, anger or sadness in regard to this change. See it swirling up as gray smoke to be absorbed by divine light. If you are having trouble with this imagery, call upon your angels and guides to help you. Then imagine them suddenly standing all around you with love and concern radiating toward you. All the negative feelings dissolve into bright white light. Feel the relief as that burden is lifted from your soul. Allow yourself to see good resulting from the change.

The number four can bring to you experiences regarding **your job or career.** Take a slow deep breath and allow your guide to show to you an experience you still recall with emotional pain attached. Hold it in your mind. Feel the pain.

Now feel angelic lights all around you, flooding that darkness with brilliant light. Feel that burden being released from your soul. Feel the joy as a spark of divine love blooms within you.

Breathe deeply and relax. Know your guardian angel is present beside you. These visualizations of unhappy episodes in your life may need to be spaced a day apart. Listen to your own divine guidance. And yet, we encourage you to do the inner cleansing of those stuck emotions that will continue to bring forth new events of like kind until you are able to rise above them and move on.

The number three now brings its vibration of creativity. Have you acted on the creative ideas sent to you? Or did you dismiss them as not being possible—or too expensive—or not having enough time to create them? Recall one of those aborted ideas and imagine what it might have looked like had you allowed it to be born. Now release it into the light.

Take time to praise yourself for all the wonderful and beautiful things you have brought into your world. Make a joyful list of your favorite things.

The number two vibrates with all the memories of partnerships and relationships. As they parade across your life's stage, pretend to sit in the audience and watch this procession. Who is the first to enter from stage right? If this person gives you joy, give him or her cheers and applause and grateful thanks.

If a person who has caused you pain merges from stage right have him/her pause and vividly recall one incident as an example of this emotional discomfort. Feel the pain, the sorrow, the confusion and anger this relationship caused.

Now, see them all alone with a spotlight shining down upon them with angels surrounding them and transforming any attached negative energy into blinding divine light. See the person being lifted up by angels and disappearing from your sight. Know you are released from all negative residues created by this relationship. You are now free to rejoice in this relationship's completion. You are now released of any Karmic tie in future lifetimes.

Number One vibrates to new beginnings. As you contemplate the past, know you have gained knowledge and wisdom from each experience. Know you no longer need to feel the negative energy from it. Release it and let it go. Fill the space with a growing joy of a burden being lifted. Smile. Breathe deeply. Feel your energy lifting as your consciousness rises into the joy of being free of any uncomfortable energy from the past.

As you study the emotional levels of consciousness, make a list of the ones you find yourself experiencing most often. Are you a pessimist or an optimist? Do you look at life and expect something bad to happen? Or do you look for good in each experience?

Spend a day in observation of how many times your thoughts turned negative. Keep a scorecard in a small notebook in your pocket. Observe how you felt within the state of fear or doubt or anxiety. Challenge yourself to recognize the negative energy and to immediately choose the energy of love. What would that look and feel like? Give an imaginary scenario.

When you have released all the negative memories still having a hold on you, you will have elevated your consciousness. Bask in the total unconditional love you are now receiving.

Meditation # 3
The Emerald Forest

Raphael will again be your guide for this meditation. Since he is of the healing green ray, a green forest is only appropriate.

Imagine us as a large being of divine light sparkling like millions of emeralds. We can wear wings if you wish. We can be either in a male or female form.

We will leave a space using ***** to allow you to write descriptive words to describe your vision.

Draw in a slow, cleansing breath and as you exhale, see your many cares and concerns slip away on each breath. They become absorbed by the divine energy of love now cloaking you in a protective shield.

Describe this shield.

*****

You are safe. You are being filled with divine joy, peace, harmony and love.

Relax your body as you breathe deeply and let go of your Beta mind's constant prattle. Allow yourself to slowly drift into the semi-conscious state of the Alpha mind.

*****

You now find yourself in a scented forest of evergreen trees twinkling with tiny lights as if in a joyous celebration. You have entered the Emerald Forest of healing green energy.

All your cares and thoughts vaporize into bliss.

Taking your hand, we lead you through the forest on a wide path that opens before you. Describe the path beneath your feet. Write down your description of the path. What does it feel like under your feet?

*****

You suddenly become aware of sounds and smells as you feel the warm, comforting air gently embrace you. You hear birds singing. You feel the path beneath your feet and breathe in the wonderful scent of pine.

*****

There are other trees mixed with the pines: large old oaks, fruit trees, maple trees, and any trees native to your home. Identify them. Allow each to bring a message to you.

*****

Nothing is said until we come to a river's edge. Describe the river.

*****

As you go deeper into the scene, it becomes more and more real in your imagination. Allow it to come alive. See the scene with your inner eyes as if you are watching a beautiful television program on nature.

*****

Which direction does the river flow? Describe the river as vividly as you can. Relax and allow your imagination to take over. Describe the bank where you stand. Take your time. Remember your descriptive words will give you additional messages after your journey.

*****

We turn to you and hand you a box with a lid on it. We instruct you to remove the lid and place your greatest concern within the box. Take your time to decide what that might be.

*****

When you are ready, we replace the lid and give the box back to you to place in the water.

Observe which way the box goes—or if it stays in place. We will decipher this action at the end of the visualization. Stay with us in this moment.

*****

Now look down at what you are wearing. Describe it.

We take your hand and with a slight lifting of air we both float across the river to the other side where there is a table with a goblet on it. Describe in detail the table, its color, texture, and shape. Describe the goblet's shape, texture and color.

We hand you the goblet now filled with a liquid. Describe the contents. As you drink this transforming elixir, describe your body's immediate reaction.

*****

Look now at what you are wearing. Describe your garment of transformation. It now reflects your eventual glorified body when you will no longer need to be in a physical form. Feel the joyous freedom of this body. Feel the total release from anything negative or fearful. Feel divine love embracing you. Rejoice in this glorious feeling of your true self.

Relax and feel this energy for a few moments.

*****

All too soon, we again take your hand and lift you across the river where you find yourself back in your regular clothes.

Still holding your hand we lead you back through the Emerald Forest where a songbird causes you to pause and look up.

Describe the bird. Using your imagination you can discern the meaning of its song. Pause, breathe, and let go of what you may think you **should see** and let it be a message from God.

*****

Now you thank the bird and move on. You are surrounded by fresh warm air and the soothing peace of the forest.

A small animal stops beside the path to sit up and speak to you. See the spirit of this animal as symbolic of its message as you describe its physical appearance and its unique personality. Breathe slowly and deeply. Relax and allow your imagination to open. Know what you see, sense, hear and know is real.

*****

Then, thank the animal for its message and move on.

*****

We remind you that all images and messages in this inner sanctuary will always be positive. Nothing negative is allowed.

A larger animal approaches and bows its head to you. Describe the animal... and write down its message... and then thank it as you move on.

*****

At the edge of the Emerald Forest, you see an open field filled with wildflowers basking in the warmth of bright sunshine. Feel the warmth of the sun and the wonderful scent coming from these flowers. What kind are they? If you don't know the name, describe its shape and color.

Pick one and bring it closer to observe every magnificent part of it. Feel the velvet of its petals. Smell its fragrance. Breathe in the essence of God within it.

Does it also have a message for you?

*****

Now as you return to your Inner Sanctuary, every experience you have had will be remembered in detail. We will use this method to send messages to you in the future. Take time to sit and meditate within your inner sanctuary that is filled with wonderful wisdom waiting for you to decode.

Remember you have a guardian angel who is always with you, ready to inspire you with answers to your questions. Relax and allow the answers to be images rather than words.

With your scientific journal, use the following gentle suggestions below to help you reap all you can from this meditation:

Green forest: Did your inner sense of smell bring a wonderful aroma of pine? Could your inner vision clearly see different kinds of trees? Write your impression of the message each tree might give if it also could have spoken to you. Use its characteristics such as an old oak having wisdom and strength and longevity.

Bird: What message did the bird bring to you? For example, if it was a **bluebird**, which symbolizes happiness, perhaps your message was encouraging you to raise your consciousness to bring you increased happiness.

Or if your bird was an eagle, you may interpret it to mean a symbol for God like the native Americans did, or it could mean clear sightedness, or it may remind you to soar above all the chaos of life and enjoy true freedom by way of your Inner Sanctuary. Allow your guides to bring you the true message for you.

Small animal: Look at your small animal's character (as well as your description of its body), as if you were making a cartoon character and the animal had a personality. For example, if it was a squirrel, are you squirrelling away food for the winter? Is this symbolic that you may be hoarding in any way? Or are you flitting here and there in a frantic effort to take care of everyday business and are maybe losing your inner peace and calm to do so?

If it was a rabbit, would you describe yourself as gentle and soft, but at times timid and skittish, afraid of your shadow? Take your time to breathe, relax and allow your guide to help.

Remember that this is given with great love and is never negative although it may point out how you can get stuck in a negative thought form.

Large animal: What was the message this animal gave to you? For example, if it is a large brown bear, it may be acting as your protector. Sometimes you may be given a flash of him standing up on his hind legs ready to charge anyone or anything trying to harm you. Let it be a gift to encourage you to stand up for yourself.

Archangel Raphael as your guide: Did you feel the unconditional love radiating from us as we spoke with you? When you asked questions, did you get a glimmer of an answer? Sometimes you may not hear words but you may be sent an idea, or a picture or some form of non-verbal communication. Learn to recognize messages given telepathically. Write down the interpretation of what you received.

Water: Water is often symbolic of life-giving spirit. If your **river** was **flowing** to the right, you are likely focusing upon the future. If it flowed to the left, you may have concerns regarding the past.

Box: Did the description of your box give you any insights? If it was made of metal, it might match a heavy concern you put into it. You might believe it could not float. Did it? (It could float because the laws of nature do not apply in your Sanctuary.). If your box floated to the **left**, it could mean your concern relates to a past experience creating the now. If it floated to the **right**, it could mean you will have to deal with it in the future. If it **stayed** right in front of you, it could mean you need to deal with it right now.

The crossing over the river is symbolic of crossing over into death where your spirit emerges free of your physical body's cares and concerns.

The goblet: If it was made of metal, go to the chapter where the symbols of metals are described. If it was made of wood, there is also an interpretation for wood. **Your first interpretation is the most valuable!**

Ponder if the goblet had any carvings on it. Ask your angel for help in interpreting the meanings.

The liquid: How did you describe it? Does the description give you a clue about its substance? How did you react to the idea of drinking an unknown substance? If you registered any fear, you had bounced back up into your conscious Beta mind. But if you allowed yourself to love and trust and stayed within the Alpha, this liquid transformed you. Could you feel it? Describe what you felt.

The return to the other side of the river is symbolic of returning from death. While on the other side, you were shown your glorified body. When you crossed over again and were back in your normal physical body, did you also de-code that symbolism? Many speak of near-death experiences where they went to heaven and were filled with unconditional love. Did you also feel that?

The field of flowers was symbolic of the path you will take from this moment forward. Whatever the meaning of these flowers represented to you it can be a message of what going forward in your life may look like.

We remind you that these guided meditations can be repeated at any time giving different visions as they relate to your present-day circumstances.

Meditation # 4
The White Stairway

*Imagine you are standing before a large white staircase. Breathe deeply and relax your body. Allow yourself to **see and feel** each step as you ascend into a higher and higher awareness in order to enter your Inner Sanctuary.*

As you step upon the first step, it turns on a bright red light that enters through your feet and travels all the way up to the top of your head and back down again.

Recall any anxiety or fears you may have had regarding finances, sexual relationships, job or career. Imagine you are dropping all concerns one by one on this first step. Watch them go "Poof!" and disappear.

Say silently or aloud, "I am brave. I easily speak up for my needs that are met each day."

As you move up to the second step, it lights up with a bright orange beam that enters through your feet and travels all the way up to the top of your head...and back through you once again.

Place on this step any doubts or fears regarding your spiritual growth or your ability to create the desires of your heart.

Say silently or aloud, "I am a spiritual being having a physical experience. I am a being of light. God and I are one."

When you move up to the next step, it turns on a bright yellow light that flows up through your body and right out the top of your head, flowing all around you and back into the step.

The yellow light enhances your mental ability to solve problems and to know what you need to know. It connects you to the Divine Mind where all your mental and emotional needs are met.

Place on this step any emotional pain you have experienced either in the past or the present. Feel it disappear. Say silently or aloud, "All my anxieties and fears are being washed out of my body with this bright yellow light of God. I am released from all emotional pain in body, mind and relationships. All anger and frustrations are now dissolved and washed clean."

Move up to the next step where a brilliant green light turns on and sends its healing energy flowing up through your body, swirling around your organs, moving up through your head and into your sinuses, out the top of your head and it then flows all around you and quietly slides back into the step.

Place on this step all concerns you may have about being loved or being lovable, of being beautiful, handsome and attractive to the opposite sex. Put away all self-doubt and self-deprecation regarding your physical body and how others see you.

Say silently or aloud, "My body rejoices in this healing light of God. It heals all relationships and brings me peace and unconditional love."

Move up to the next step and watch a beautiful pale blue light turn on. Feel its energy swirl up through and around your body, lifting you into bliss. Feel it slowly rise out the top of your head taking with it all past confrontations, anger, disappointments, misunderstandings, and miscommunications. Watch the blue light absorb it and know that no negative beliefs or concerns about communication have any impact upon you.

Say silently or aloud, "I am able to communicate my deepest feelings and concerns with calm and clarity." Watch as this healing light flows all around you and then slips back into the step.

As you move up to the sixth step, it immediately winks on with a deep indigo, bluish-purple light. You feel as if you are walking among the stars.

On this step, place all your anxieties about making mistakes. You drop upon this step all your fears of looking foolish by what you say or do. Drop all past so-called foolish mistakes in this step. Then let go of any fears that your extra-sensory perceptions may be wrong. You allow them to sharpen and fill you with confidence that you are able to sense other people's feelings, that you can see the past, present and future, that you are developing and appreciating all your inner senses.

Say, "All my inner senses are awakening now. I see with inner sight. I can hear my angels and guides clearly. I sense what to do each moment. I know with certainty what I am to do at any given moment. I can call upon my angels and guides to open my inner awareness and inspire me with creative ideas for solving problems, for gaining insight and information when I need it."

Move up to the top step now and bask in the lovely violet-purple light that gathers its energy around your feet and slowly moves up throughout your body, blessing it with a new spiritual awakening.

On this step, place any confusing beliefs about God and the hereafter. Put away any fear of a God who punishes "sins" and "errors." See the fear and misperceptions slowly disappear.

Say silently or aloud, "I embrace my God who is non-judgmental and all loving. My Creator fills me now with pure love, peace, harmony, laughter and joy. I rejoice in this."

At the top landing, there is a door. Describe it in detail. Where is the handle? What is the door made of? How tall is it? Use as many descriptive words as you can. Your interpretation later will bring you insights that may amaze you.

*****

Open your door and step into your inner sanctuary that you have created, visualizing all the most beautiful places in nature that you can see within your memory and mind.

Describe them now in detail: the trees; the different kinds and colors of flowers; the water; and your guardian angel who is always there waiting to speak with you.

Take your time in doing this. Allow yourself to let go of preconceived ideas. Allow this inner space to become the Kingdom of Heaven within you.

Imagine now the Archangel Gabriel with its pure blue light of the gift of clear communication of ideas. It opens its arms to you. Without hesitation, you walk into that embrace of pure, unconditional love. You feel the radiance of God's powerful sky-blue energy engulfing you, inspiring you, lifting you into pure bliss. Remain in that embrace and allow yourself to be inspired and filled with divine bliss.

Gabriel hands you a lovely pale blue flower from your nearby garden. Describe the flower, its texture, and smell. The archangel shows you how the color reflects the energy center in your throat that needs healing. Imagine you are now in a special laboratory where your holographic image is presented in front of you. Your body and spirit are revealed in full color.

Do not judge your body. Reflect with joy how it has served you well.

Gabriel points out any blockages within your meridians and shows you the emotional energy that is the cause. If you are expressing any fear and anxiety regarding your ability to express your feelings and ideas, this purifying blue light now cleanses and heals it and frees your gifts of expression.

With a gentle smile, the archangel hands you a tiny brush where you can clean out your body's arteries and clean out any of your meridians. Do this joyously and playfully and with great intent of purpose to heal your body.

With the necessary tools at your disposal, you are allowed to work on removing any blockages of fear wherever pain resides. See the archangel hand you a glowing jar of pure sparkling white energy. You rub it on the pain and feel it move into your body with a glowing warmth. You see your body repairing itself.

Know now that your body is repairing itself.

*****

Like a little child, you clap your hands and dance a little jig in appreciation.

Gabriel smiles and with gentle words given telepathically, this beautiful archangel relates how you can continue to improve your mental, spiritual, emotional and physical health. You are now free to express your needs in every way God inspires you to do so.

We understand how with this healing meditation, it would be so easy to be skeptical and allow doubt to abort the healing. And yet, we say unto you, always ask for your highest and greatest good. If it is for healing, it shall be so. If it is not, it will not happen. Trust the divine plan is always unfolding perfectly.

Meditation #5
The Spaceship

Begin your preparation for this deep meditation by relaxing your body, breathing deeply, and visualizing yourself in your Inner Sanctuary. Feel it. See it. Know it is your special place right inside you.

Breathe in the beauty and peace and relax for a moment or two.

Then, imagine the Archangel Uriel is appearing before you. It glows with a brilliant golden aura. It offers its hand for you to join it on a quiet walk. You gladly accept the offer and find yourself on a country road with sand at your feet. The smell of saltwater comes from somewhere to your left and the warm sun beams down upon you on this bright and beautiful day.

"Where are we going?" you ask.

"Just a little way ahead," says the archangel. "But first you must let go of the heavy burden you are carrying."

You are confused because you didn't even bring a wallet with you. "What burden?" you ask.

"Your concerns for another."

Oh! And you remember how you've been worrying about someone. You sigh and are instantly shown how that person is surrounded by angels. You nod and let go.

"Okay," you say, "Now am I okay?"

"Not yet," says the archangel. "You are weighed down with worry that not enough of your desires are being met because of finances."

You sigh and nod and wait because you just know there is likely something else that is weighing you down—that you have ignored so as not to get too depressed.

"Let go of all your concerns over relationships."

You release a long sigh. So, okay, you were hiding one or two concerns in that regard.

"Now am I okay?" you ask.

"You are still too heavily laden," says Uriel.

You and the archangel walk together for a while in silence while you ponder what on earth the angel could be thinking. Suddenly, you become aware of other negative emotions popping into your mind. Anger, frustration and impatience with people who never seem to "get it" all start to overwhelm you. You wonder how you can ever let them go.

You walk in silence with this amazing being of light.

As you breathe deeply, you find that with each step you feel lighter and lighter. All thoughts and concerns of your life on earth seem to slowly disappear.

You reach a curve in the road and as you turn the corner, you see a shiny spaceship made of clear crystal.

"It's beautiful!" you exclaim.

"It is yours," says the large being of golden light. "It cannot carry a heavy load. This is why we have asked you to let go of any negative thoughts or anxieties."

The hatch on the tiny ship opens and a ladder tumbles out. You climb in without a backward glance.

Uriel remains nearby, instructing you in what each of the instruments mean. "You have a wide-lens camera that will zoom into any city within any country. You can listen to conversations wherever there is conflict and with this large green button, you can spread the area with a coat of pink energy to lift the consciousness out of strife and into a peaceful conclusion to conflict.

"Ha!" you exclaim. "I'm seeing me spreading a coat of that pink antacid medicine so people can heal their inability to accept another's point of view and find a peaceful solution."

You sit in front of the small well-lit console and wonder what each button or gauge means.

Uriel continues with instructions. "With the beam of light beneath your ship, you can turn dark thoughts into light ones, prejudice and bigotry into tolerance, and hate into love."

"Wow! That's amazing!" you say. Once more you check out the other dials and buttons and now seem to know exactly what each means.

"I'm ready to go," you say.

"And where will you go?" asks the archangel.

"I will go to the offices of my government and unscramble the conflict between the people who represent our country so they can come together to bring justice and peace to our people."

You pause quite pleased with yourself. "Then I will..."

"Dear one," says Uriel, "you must obey the law of non-interference."

"What?" you cry. "What good is all of this if I cannot use it?"

"Ah, but you can. Know it has to be freely given with no intent to do harm and no desire to fill your own emotional needs for justice or revenge."

You have to think about that for a moment or two. "Well, okay. I understand... I think... but if I cannot change things, what good is it?"

"You can only send inspirational messages through your vision of good. Those who capture the idea will then decide to implement it... or not."

"Huh," You think about that for a moment. "What if no one agrees to make the changes for good that I am sending?"

"Oh, but many will receive the inspiration and will find a way to act upon it. Keep sending that beam of divine light to lift your fellow beings out of darkness and into light. They will receive you with gladness and joy."

Uriel folds up the small stairway and closes the hatch on your spaceship. It steps back and watches you lift off and zoom away. Your mission has now been established. You have the amazing tools of your inner senses for creating peace and harmony within your private world and within the entire planet. Even global warming can now be solved as you send light and joy to awaken some genius minds who will find many solutions.

Meditation # 6
On an Intimate Relationship

Many people ask us when they will meet their soulmate. We have discussed this in a previous chapter, but now we will give you a meditation on the subject. If your Council of Elders believes it is part of God's divine plan for your life, and you believe you are ready for an intimate relationship, use this meditation to create the perfect one.

Begin with deep breathing as you consciously relax your body to prepare yourself for meditation. When you are comfortable and able to visualize your Inner Sanctuary, take a few moments to relax there and unwind. Breathe in the glorious atmosphere of your magnificent garden. Hear the music of the water you have envisioned. Smell the sweet aroma of your flower garden. Feel the warmth of a perfect sunny day. Relax and let go of all other thoughts.

Imagine now that you are greeted by your spirit counselor who is the archangel Michael. Feel the presence of this magnificent being of red light. Feel its perfect love for you as it guides you to your resting place and sits down beside you. It knows your heart's desires.

Pull your breath in slowly and watch a bright ruby-red energy flow from this messenger of God through the top of your head downward throughout all of your body. As you release the breath, imagine all your concerns about relationships are being washed from your body and out your fingers and toes.

Now imagine yourself as God's Lamplighter of old with a long wand ignited with a divine spark. See yourself igniting souls wherever you encounter them. Imagine them turning a frown into a smile. See their aura growing brighter.

Begin a conversation with your soul in your journal. **Use your imagination.** *Let go of fear and doubt in your ability to do this. Your soul is a giant being of light but it is not God. Your soul has vast knowledge but not all knowledge. Do not look to your soul for visions of the future. As you continue to listen for your soul's response, you will hear that small inner voice as a yearning to communicate with you. Open your mind and heart to bond in this relationship. It may be the most valuable encounter of your entire life.*

Hold fast to the visions that come to you while in your Inner Sanctuary. It is here that God can send messages to you more easily. Trust and believe these things are real... and you will experience the joy of being heard, understood and loved unconditionally.

Now ask your soul if it is time for you to join with another soul in an intimate relationship. Breathe deeply and sense the answer. You may receive it in a picture of a partner either in the form of a human or of a being of light. You will know.

Then ask what you need to do to create this relationship. You may be given ideas such as places to go where meeting new people is possible. Or you may be just told to wait as this person will come to you. Or you may be told to wait and allow God to present this person to you in the perfect timing for your soul.

We remind you to acknowledge the desires of your heart as they are presented to you by God. Always ask for clarification in what to do next. Then wait for an inspiration leading you to the next step. Let go and allow Michael the time and space to do his matchmaking magic.

The archangel reminds you that when seeking a compatible relationship, look for someone who matches your soul age and complements your soul's vibrational energy as well as having the same intellection interests. Look for someone without emotional ties to another or having financial challenges. Review the description of the soul personalities and their point of view of the world. It will help you discern what color soul you are dealing with. Then you may need to review soul phases of growth to know how to work with beginner souls and how to avoid them as a love partner. Be wary of those who seek physical satisfaction before getting to know you as a complex being of light—as an ensouled being.

We need to remind you: your Council of Elders has already selected various souls to grace your story with opportunities not only for a happy relationship, but for the joy of having a challenge to keep you alert and advancing.

Rejoice! Be glad in all your encounters with other souls. Seek to see the best in all the people you meet. If you find discord while with another, turn it into harmony... or walk away.

And if your Council decides you need to meet and begin a personal relationship with someone from a past lifetime, know this group of wise old souls will support you every step of the way.

Your Council and all the archangels are only seeking your highest and greatest good. Be at peace in knowing this is so. You are always guided with perfect love and support from these elders as well as an army of angels.

Chapter 21
What Happens When I Die?

Your spirit lives on.

While your spirit detaches from your physical body each night, death is the final detachment from the physical world. When death nears, fear may prevent the spirit from leaving. The physical mind may cling to the spirit and refuse to let it go. Fears surrounding death come from preconceived ideas of a judgment that could send you to hell or create a fear of letting go of a loved one. It can trap a spirit within a body that no longer serves you.

We always encourage you to let go of any fear of death or the process of dying. You have done it many times before. Souls declare that the birth process is far more traumatic than the dying process. We understand your fear of pain and how you relate that with death. We say unto you: each soul's spirit entity will experience pain and discomfort in their physical body in some form or another all throughout the life. You cannot escape the challenges to your soul's physical, mental, emotional and spiritual selves.

While the soul realizes that it is gaining new knowledge and wisdom as it moves through life's successes or failures, the spirit does not. The soul knows that an experience which the spirit or the conscious mind may consider a failure or a waste of time or of little value, the soul sees it as a step forward on its journey toward enlightenment. When your spirit has its life review, it will see the value of its deepest emotional involvements. It will not find any judgement regarding its choices. Your Council will help you see those choices from God's perspective of non-judgment and your angels will help you gain the gift of wisdom from every decision you have ever made.

During your life, we urge you to see each choice as a rough gem that can be cut and polished into great value.

The Vortex of Ascension

When the human entity no longer needs its physical form, the soul sheds it and leaves with its spirit to go through the process of death. It rises from the non-functioning body and immediately goes through what is called the *Vortex of Ascension*. People who have returned from a near-death experience refer to it as "the tunnel" where they experience a vibrational pulling toward a bright light—thus the saying, "The light at the end of the tunnel." This process helps the spirit detach from all concerns about leaving loved ones behind. At the end of this tunnel it becomes a light body or a glorified body.

Thus begins your life in your spirit form, which we state again is as an exact duplicate of your physical body. This faster-vibrating body can sometimes linger on Earth, hovering over its physical body, refusing to leave.

This is why making the connection between you and your soul is so important. This is why you sometimes have had a feeling you have been in a place or situation before. By listening to your soul, you can save yourself a great deal of unwanted consequences of your choices.

A natural growth in spirit consciousness guides the soul with its spiritual partner through a life review. While some may call this review a soul's Karma, it is simply the progress of viewing the soul's trials and errors while living a sentient life from the beginning levels through an intermediate phase and into advanced maturity.

There is no judgment of this natural development of the soul, nor are there consequences except to become aware of what it has created within the physical experience. This explains why God does not judge the soul when it is exploring the physical dimension, nor does God need to create any after-life consequences of a hell.

Your life review expands your spirit's knowledge and awareness after death. God reveals to you through a life review all your words and deeds, thoughts and dreams from your very first beginnings of your life. Some call God's mind the Akashic Records. Few select people have permission to tap into that divine memory. Yet, for your spirit's advancement, all is revealed to you in detail at the end of your soul's journey.

Near-Death Experiences

When a soul is declared dead and goes to the other side but is told it must return to physical life, this is not as uncommon an experience as you might believe. Your Council may set up a deadly accident that would offer an opportunity for the spirit and soul to gain a quantum leap in divine wisdom.

Many people have told their stories of dying and going to heaven. Each story may vary but they are similar in how the doctors observe the loss of a heartbeat and clinically declare the patient dead. The person's spirit rises from the physical body but does not proceed through a the Vortex of Ascension. They will meet with an angel or a loved one who speaks with them of their life so far and then says they have to return. Most do not want to leave the peace and serenity of what they often call "Heaven."

These are now called "Near Death Experiences" or NDEs. If you have not done so already, we encourage you to become aware of other near-death experiences as this knowledge will decrease your fear of death both for yourself and for your loved ones. Death is merely the transition from the physical life into the world of spirit. Some feel it is a "coming home" celebration when you meet those loved ones who have gone before you.

The spirit's trip to the next dimension gives the soul and its human partner the opportunity to learn of life beyond the physical. In this next dimension you may be shown your life story so far. You decide if it was valuable or not and then ask you what you might like to do if you were given more time on Earth. When these heavenly beings tell you that you have to return, you may be reluctant to leave such a peaceful place. They will encourage you to share this other-worldly experience with others.

Another gift in near-death experiences can be a surrendering of your attachments to the physical life and trusting God's divine plan for your next departure time. These rare experiences cause the human to be free of any fear of death.

Your Council is always monitoring your life to guide and help you with the divine plan as set forth by God for your excursions into the physical world.

While your soul and council may even set up a gene in your DNA such as cancer that could be the eventual opportunity for your return home, you may use the challenge and survive. The gift of any disease or threat of death is in how you use it. Do you choose to grumble and complain? Or do you smile through the pain, do whatever you can to relieve it and move on? It is always your moment-by-moment choice. Each choice builds upon the previous one and each experience expands your soul's growth toward oneness with God.

Suicide

When an entity contemplates suicide, alarm bells sound. God sends angels and advisors to help lift the person out of the darkness of those thoughts **for suicide only turns the soul around and sends it right back** into the same circumstances in the next life. Understandably, when pain is more than the person's spirit can handle, an exit through suicide may be the sought-after relief. Again, we say God's infinite compassion never judges the soul's choices. It knows only experience can teach the soul to make better choices in the next incarnation.

While the taking of one's life is not a good choice, we again say there is no judgment from God or from the person's council. Instead, there is love and patience. If the human believes suicide to be a sin, they may find themselves in the Between World where their fears of punishment may be experienced. **Your long-held beliefs are powerful and can create your afterlife.**

After a time of rest and healing, the council will then help the soul plan another lifetime where the story repeats the dilemma that brought them to choose suicide. The difference will be a vague memory that suicide did not gain them the necessary escape from their challenges and hopefully they will make the wiser choice to stay and gain wisdom from the experience of deep depression or horrific pain. For only by facing one's life experiences with courage and determination to make it better can it be for the soul's greatest advancement. It is always a matter of rising above fear and anxiety.

Your Council of Elders is the translator of the mind of God as to your soul's plan. Your purpose as an explorer of planet Earth is to gain the greatest knowledge and wisdom from the expedition. God is in constant awareness of your soul's thoughts and emotions.

Sometimes a soul may shrink from incarnating again if it has returned from a particularly difficult lifetime. God is patient and kind and understanding. It will never force the soul to incarnate. It will encourage the soul to continue to study the physical world through another incarnation. Perhaps one hundred of Earth's years may pass before the soul resumes its studies for it will never progress in learning the art of creating without experiencing sentient life on a physical planet. A hundred years may seem like only a few hours within the spirit realm.

We need not remind you that each new life within that cycle begins with a birth and ends with a death. Humans fear death because they are not aware of the bigger picture of their soul life.

Is it possible for a human to be born without a soul?

No, it is not. A soul is the life-breath within a physical body. Without a soul, the body cannot survive.

At the moment of birth, the soul entered your human body as a particle of itself in the form we call your spirit. Much of the new human's awareness of its soul depends upon its number of previous lifetimes within the physical dimension and how much wisdom has been gained from each life experience.

Beginner souls do not know their human personality. It has no conscious awareness of itself, the soul or of God because their soul has had no previous experience to call upon. Only through the sentient-life experiences within the physical world does the soul grow in understanding the consequences of the choices it makes as their physical vehicle of expression.

Try to remember that life and death within the human drama is only part of the soul's story. The human costume wears out with age because of the pull of gravity and the ingestion of foods that can deplete the body's energy with the results sometimes bringing about illness.

When your council helps your soul select the DNA from your parents, some recessive genes that can lead to your exit off the planet may be part of the package through illness such as cancer or other debilitating disease. Each exit offers a wondrous opportunity for releasing fear by rising above all negative feelings to soar with the angels and be an inspiration for all who walk with you.

We remind you again of your gift of free will that allows you to change a situation by making a different choice. You make thousands of decisions each day from what time to arise to when to sleep, what to wear and what to eat and so forth. Each seemingly small choice is always a building block of your future. The outfit you choose this day may bring you a needed compliment. You may have been inspired to choose it, but if you chose another outfit instead you may not have received the compliment. You would not have known the difference.

What about Karma?

Karma speaks to the concept of balance. All things will become balanced sooner or later. It is the natural order of things.

You come back again and again because you are an apprentice under the Master Creator studying a physical world. You committed to an entire cycle of lives to fulfil your contract.

Each time your soul returns with a new body and a new story, it excitedly looks forward to the adventures it will encounter. Like any good story, it knows its leading character will face challenges. You have been returning to your planet again and again over eons of time growing with knowledge and wisdom.

Contrary to some beliefs, incarnating is a privilege not a punishment. For those of you who may be experiencing a life of sorrow and pain, of mistreatment from others, be assured that we are here to assist and uplift you out of the darkness and into the light. All experiences within your physical world have a golden nugget of wisdom worth far more value than any mineral within your planet. God would never limit your soul's choice to explore.

Most souls love coming to Earth to tell their stories. They are the author of their stage play as well as the leading character, director, and producer using moment by moment inspiration to make the story come alive by expressing passion and excitement.

Ah! Yes. You may say that some soul's stories are horrendous. Still we say unto you: the bigger picture reveals the reasons behind each story for it is always a balancing of emotions so you can experience all of the challenges and joys of your planet's polarities.

From the human perspective, this may seem to be inhumane. Some may ask how God can allow such evil to exist. Understand God does not interfere with a soul's life or else your story would not be beneficial. First-hand experiences are, indeed, the best teacher. Your soul does not tell its story—you, as its leading character tell the story. Your soul is more of an observer of your life while at the same time it is the director and producer of your play.

Therefore, we encourage you to become acquainted with your spirit duplicate that holds all your desires and beliefs through which you create. We encourage you to document your emotions. They are the keys that unlock your treasure chest of success and happiness.

Your soul gains wisdom from each act you do and from each emotion you express. It loves watching its lead character. It never knows what you will do next, especially in the beginning lifetimes when you and your soul barely communicate with one another.

After your story ends on Earth, your spirit continues telling your story in the next dimension that people call Heaven. It leaves behind all stress and fears as it enters this higher vibrating world where there is only love. This heaven-like dimension becomes an amazing experience of manifesting every desire with only a thought.

When your sojourn in this heavenly place has gained your soul all that it can, it then incorporates your spirit body within itself like an actor who has had a good long run in an award-winning play and finally retires. It then returns home to share its awards with all of its soul friends.

We remind you: while you are within a physical world, your soul's script is wide open for change. The task is for your spirit to communicate with your soul so as to work together to become a master creator of God's beauty and goodness.

Indeed, we say unto you, each action your spirit takes, each emotion it expresses becomes the background music of your play on Earth's stage. Without the music the story would be dull and disappointing.

Do I have to make up for every mistake I ever made?

Dear soul: we repeat that all of life within the physical is seeking balance. The story your soul tells often spills over into the next lifetime in order to bring about balance.

For example, if a person dies while still addicted to a substance, the law of balance will require the soul to bring back an addiction in the next lifetime to offer the soul an opportunity to overcome it.

There is the saying, "The Ties That Bind." There are at times literal strings attached from one soul to another. These strings hold a past life story that sets up a connection in the next life. Of course, these connections, although energy related, vibrate too quickly to be seen by the naked eye. In the spirit body, it is like a string attached from one umbilical cord to another. Some intuitive people can sense it and say, "He has strings attached to that person."

Many define this as Karma but let us give a different perspective of those ties that bind. You do not return as some believe to mend mistakes. Rather your soul returns for the sheer joy of creating a story to act out on Earth's stage. This is an amazing opportunity to gather God's creative powers for exploring new adventures or for watching your entity play the leading role of the story your soul has written.

Although, as we had said previously, a new planet has been created to sustain sentient life where souls who vacate this planet will finish their cycle of incarnations on this new planet. It is as on your Earth where souls will have polarities to learn balance.

The strings that bind you to another soul's story are planned whenever a previous lifetime ended with unfinished business. Only by reincarnating with a soul who is enlisted as part of your soul's story can the soul advance.

I am reminded of the movie "When Dreams May Come." The leading man, played by Robin Williams, takes on the role of a man who died and found himself in a strange reality that brought him joy until he remembered how his wife had committed suicide. His determination to find her takes him into his beliefs of hell and purgatory. His powerful love for her moves him beyond his beliefs. Here is a beautiful example of the afterlife according to one's belief system. It also shows how two souls can plan a future life together.

What about the Concept of Time?

In the afterlife, you leave behind time and space and the polarities of your physical Earth.

While you are experiencing the dense energy of your planet, you must deal with the concept of gravity, time and space. It can become a real challenge creating the feelings of never having enough time, or the opposite of feeling the agony of time never releasing you from physical pain and suffering.

This is one of the dominant challenges of your planet Earth. With its denser, slower vibration, time is fixed according to your planet's path around your sun. And yet for you, as a sentient being, time can be flexible according to your spirit's emotional view of it. It may seem to go slow when you are anxious and then fast when you are joyful. The miracle of this dense energy is in how you can look backward and evaluate your creations and then look forward in determining how you can improve upon them.

Remember: Time is only measured by your clocks and calendars—not by your spirit or soul.

Your lifespan upon your planet is always flexible. Your soul may plan more than one possible death, but if there is a change in circumstances at the time planned, your soul may choose to survive even a technically declared death experience. These stories are life changing not only in themselves but for all who hear of their experience. What they encountered during the death process awakens them to the knowledge of their spirit's existence after death and they no longer fear that grand exit but instead gain a great reverence for their new perspective on the next life after death.

What about "Walk-ins" I understand that when one soul's physical body is still perfectly good and yet they decide to leave the planet, another soul may create a spirit duplicate of that body and exchange places with them. We call the new soul a "Walk-in." Are we understanding that concept correctly?

Indeed, you are. While this experience is now widely known, it is happening more and more as your planet evolves. People surrounding this phenomenon may not realize what has happened. They will note how the person who survived death now seems changed. The new soul may not like the clothes in the closet and determine to wear a different style. They may not seem to recognize people they've known for a long time. But most importantly, they may seem to have a happier outlook on life.

These are signs of a "Walk-in."

You may ask why this happens.

While there are a many reasons, the main one comes from the soul's choice to vacate the physical life without going through death. It agrees to allow another soul's spirit to take over the life-force of the body and complete the body's lifespan upon your planet. Sometimes it allows an older, more experienced soul to take over, knowing the soul can bring much good to the world.

It is a Privilege to Explore A Physical World

While some may look upon the concept of incarnation as a necessary evil, we say unto you it is a sacred privilege. Many souls who desire to play on your planet's stage cannot return during its present transition. Mother Earth has demanded that only advanced souls may incarnate until her body recovers from the many scars she has endured.

As advanced souls visit Earth again, they will witness a magical healing of all the planet's bruises and scars. You will in the near future find your planet filled with green life and clear sparkling water. Souls in the future will come and enjoy Earth as a paradise as originally designed by the Creator.

You may ask for a timeline of this prediction. For you who measure time, it would be disheartening to say it could take many years. After the present immature and destructive souls pass into spirit, young people with more mature souls will take over. There is already a surge of consciousness among the young who are now demanding of their elders to wake up to the destruction of their home planet. More young people throughout the world are taking power from those who seek only their own self-interest.

Only from your human perspective you may say you do not desire to return to the chaos of this transition. Your soul has already answered the call to return because of your love for the planet and because you agreed to help raise the consciousness of your fellow humans at this time in Earth's history.

We encourage you to hold fast within your mind the image of your planet filled with life and vitality. While in a deep meditation, this simple task has great power.

This is one purpose for your return to Earth. There are many other reasons. Look to the people closest to you. Resolve to love unconditionally both friend and foe. When it is time for you to complete this lifetime, you shall easily leave all behind and ascend into glory.

The majority of souls upon your planet in this year of 2020 are not aware of all these things we share with you. It is not your job to preach to them or to try to "save them," for they have their own guides and angels assisting them with far more knowledge and wisdom than you have regarding their life's story. And yet, when another asks for your wisdom, listen first to your angel's words and then share what you receive.

Tell us more about the "Between World."

God has prepared a place for those souls who are unaware of life after death. Many cannot let go of the emotions that tie them to a person, place or thing within your Earth plane. We call this the Between World.

I'm reminded of another movie that examines this topic. "Ghost" tells the story of a man who died violently. When his spirit was jerked out of its physical body, the man did not at first realize that he was dead until he saw his lifeless body on the road.

Most of this rendition of the afterlife is a rather accurate accounting of a soul stuck in the Between World. But it was not accurate as to how a dark soul meets its afterlife. There are no demons or dark spirits who drag them into hell.

While many upon your planet may argue that it is not right for a person to escape punishment for their grievous crimes against others, we say again there is only love for each spirit as it departs from its physical life.

We urge you to change your perspective of life in the physical. It is indeed only a story told by the soul who is safely watching the drama unfold upon Earth's stage. It loves its leading character as it plays the antagonist role in the story. It knows it plays a vital part not only for its own advancement, but for all those who enter Earth's stage and interact with their opposing character.

Observe the drama of the impeachment of the President of the United States. There was the push and pull of good versus evil, as the scales of justice tried to balance. It was a drama well played by a great many people. Some who have been asleep are now awakening to the consequences of their actions.

The Between World is merely a waiting room for the spirit to recover from the shock of leaving the physical world. A person's beliefs create the experience. If they believe they are worthy of their imagined Heaven, then they will create a world of their beliefs where they shall go until they are ready for their life review. If they believe their life's deeds warrant them hell, then it is there they shall go.

Speak more of this "Life Review" please.

With the help of your guides and angels, your spirit will view your life not only from your personal, intellectual and emotional perspective, but also from the emotional, mental and spiritual experience of anyone who has ever interacted with you. When you feel and know the other's point of view, you gain greater awareness of how sentient life is always an exchange of emotions, ideas, and concepts. And always the exchange will become apparent as to each soul's developmental stage.

This review is essential to the soul's development and growth.

As an example of the afterlife, I like to refer to the movie, "Defending Your Life," with Mel Brooks and Meryl Streep. It reveals a newly deceased spirit who must show how he has overcome his fears and is ready to move on to the next level of advancement. The key revelation came in the realization of how his fears, which were many, were the only thing keeping him from moving on with a spirit with whom he had fallen in love. Love was the motivation that moved him beyond his fears to gain him the desired advancement.

This is a perfect analogy of how powerful the emotions emanating from love can be. This concept of the power of love is precisely why we have put such emphasis on helping you become aware of your emotions and how they can either inhibit your soul's advancement or put you on a fast track.

What is Love…really?

Love is not an emotion. It is a state of being. While some would describe love as a feeling, it is not. The feelings associated with love are happiness, joy, humor, inner peace, compassion, bliss and a sense of euphoria. Unconditional love floods a being with awareness of God's presence within. With such powerful emotions associated with love, it is easy to understand why humans associate love with an emotion.

What About Good Versus Evil?

When the pendulum swings, God is directing you to look at life from a different perspective. **Viewing the negative side is just as important as seeing the positive.** The challenge here is to bring about balance.

We repeat—your soul is designed by God to be an explorer of your physical world which must include <u>both</u> of its polarities. When we say that God is the energy by which everything exists, we mean just that: God is the energy of your physical planet's dark energy. While it may be hard to accept that God is both the light and the darkness, let this be a truth that brings compassion and love for all who are caught up in what you deem as evil. And indeed, much evil is exhibited in baby souls who kill and maim, rape and steal from innocent humans.

As explorers of your physical planet that was created by God, each soul must explore all aspects of it including the dark side. Only by achieving the wisdom that God is in everyone and everything can you accept this truth.

We say unto you: <u>there is no evil</u>. It is only your label for anyone or anything that does not conform to your belief of good. While beginner souls may experiment with energy from your negative polarity, **they are not evil.** Their intent is to explore their new world and all its exciting challenges, dangers and darkness. You label the darkness as evil but in the exploration of evil, its contrast with good will reap a wisdom that will move you closer to God's perfect love and perfect acceptance. Hold fast to the knowledge that life on your planet is brief. All experiences reap the soul new knowledge which begets wisdom. Future lifetimes will reflect that wisdom.

If you can let go of your concept of judgment and the consequences of bad behavior in relation to one being either accepted into heaven or thrown into hell, perhaps you can conceive of a God who lets you write your story and even helps you perform as the leading lady or leading man **as you play the role of the antagonist**. It would be a very boring story without the main character's struggle to overcome the elements and survive, or to win the battle against an evil source and become the hero or heroine of its story.

We see your confusion of good versus evil, as well as reward versus punishment. This lies in your religious background of beliefs that God has created both a Heaven and a Hell. Only in your world does a human's need for justice thrive. It often stems from beginner soul's immature point of view.

We cannot say it often enough: You are One with God. You and all who went before you are explorers of God's worlds. Naturally, you will at times hold on to beliefs that no longer serve you. Dismiss those that no longer hold truth for you. You are older and wiser now.

You have envisioned the Creator as a benevolent ruler upon a throne. You say God created you in Its image and likeness. Rather humans have made God in **your own image and likeness.** You have made the God of Love a god of hate and divisiveness—or how else could a Hell be created?

We continually say unto you—**God does not judge you—for God is the energy of pure love dwelling within you and**

within everyone and everything. That pure love keeps Its creations alive with Its divine breath, Its divine inspiration, and Its divine wisdom. God is not human nor is It spirit. God is pure Energy. You are made up of divine energy and therefore you radiate God with every breath you breathe. We cannot repeat this often enough, dear souls.

The one called Jesus declared that you are gods! You have the power of all the divine energy to create anything your soul, your mind and your emotions can conceive and determine to manifest within your world. You are an apprentice in training under the Master Creator. Rejoice in the truth of who you really are.

Only souls who are living in a physical dimension such as your planet's polarity can experience the emotions of jealousy, anger, intolerance, bigotry, and hate. You are not judged for this for in your search for God you must taste the fruit of the Tree of Good and Evil before you discover the Tree of Life where negative emotions do not exist.

As the soul progresses through each lifetime, its light grows brighter until it becomes a beacon of light unto the world. We call them God's Lamplighters.

Yet, we say unto you: experience begets truth. God buried jewels of truth within your Earth's polarities. Excavate the jewels of divine truth as the gold and precious gems of wisdom from whatever you create physically, intellectually, spiritually and emotionally.

God is not your judge. You are.

The beauty of God's plan is that each soul learns truth only from experiencing a physical life within a physical reality. Repetition of experiences and their consequences in a hundred different ways is why you return to Earth again and again in order to grasp life's mysteries. **It is not because you have failed in any way. It is because there are too many mysteries to discover in just one trip to Earth.**

Imagine yourself as Columbus who first landed in what he thought was a New World but is now determined to be the Bahamas. When he looked over to Cuba, he thought it was mainland China. He also thought he might have landed in Japan. In truth, he thought wrong in many ways. It did not matter to his soul who continued in his beliefs to explore and discover his New World.

Indeed, dear soul, you are Columbus. Do explore your world with great enthusiasm and joy. Unlock its secrets. Do not allow fear and danger to heed your continued search for the treasures of your new land. Claim it as your home. You were created to explore a new world, to meet and interact with new people in order to gain new knowledge that helps you feel safe and comfortable.

Your goal is to rid yourself of all fear and anxiety.

This can become a real challenge if you expect others to see the world as you do. Remember that each soul not only sees their world from its unique perspective but also from its developmental stage of advancement gaining wisdom only through lifetimes of experience.

In the next chapter, we will offer to you a list of guiding principles to speed you on your exploration of planet Earth. Rejoice in all things. See good in your challenges. Give thanks for all your blessings.

Chapter 22
How Do I
Find Happiness?!

Beloved souls, we say unto you, <u>choose to be happy!</u> It is your free will to do so. Choose to examine your thoughts, your emotions, your desires and most of all, your determination to be happy. And then study our Guiding Principles and practice using them each day until they become a part of your spirit's consciousness. With these concepts, you will lift yourself out of fear of lack or loss and begin to smile more, to feel more joy. Your emotional energy tank will fill up more quickly. Your fears will diminish and you will find your health restored. Miracles can happen when you have raised your spirit's consciousness into a belief that everything is possible.

Watch your emotional fuel tank. If it is running low, take the suggestions within this book to fill it. You can begin by refueling with simple laughter. Yes. Imagine something that tickles you. If that is not easy for you, buy a book of jokes or simply laugh out loud for a full thirty seconds.

Everything is vibrating energy including your thoughts. Many spiritual teachers throughout the ages have said, "As you think, so shall it be."

We offer these guiding principles as a summary of this book. May they speed you along your path to inner peace and happiness leading to enlightenment.

Whenever your energy is running low, check your emotional fuel gauges to see if you have ignored one of these principles. Reestablish the positive mindset to refuel the energy within your body, mind, and spirit. Become aware of your emotional and intellectual states as the first step to changing what is not comfortable for you in any given moment. Only then can you choose to recharge your energy and experience pure delight and happiness.

Guiding Principle # 1: Free Will and Intent

Your Free Will is your precious gift of choice. Each day offers you hundreds of choices that require use of this principle. It is your **intent** that opens the door to your good or leads you into a challenge.

Your Intent is the "why" behind everything you choose to do. If your intent is for the greatest good for yourself and everyone concerned, then you have the power of angels to help you manifest what you desire.

If your intent is to do harm to another or to yourself, your Council will send angels to plead with you to think again. If you refuse to listen, they will help you gain wisdom from the negative outcome.

Again, God does not judge your choices. We help you turn a negative outcome into your greatest good—how else can you discern the difference?

Like attracts like. Whatever you think and believe in your heart, you shall become.

Think of your spirit as a candle in the darkness. Others will seek to match your light. If you have chosen to bring forth negative thoughts and negative emotions, you shall reap what you sow in experiencing negative people and emotions.

The focus always comes back to your beliefs. It can change a positive thought with a more dominant, negative one. If you seek a mate and yet do not believe yourself attractive enough, you have cancelled any and all affirmations of what a "Positive Mental Attitude" would achieve.

The State of Fear Versus the State of Love

Confusion versus Clarity
Chaos versus Order
Destruction versus Creation
Argument versus Discussion
Anger versus Acceptance
Hate versus Love
Envy versus Joy
Lack versus Abundance
Greed versus Generosity
Revenge versus Forgiveness
Judgment versus Detachment
Blame versus Responsibility
Darkness versus Light
Falsehood versus Truth

Guiding Principle # 2 — Maintain Balance

The Rule of Balance refers to the polarities of the planet that can throw off anyone who is either too negative or too positive. Everyone and everything must be in balance or it cannot survive.

A car may not run smoothly if the tires are out of balance. Your body cannot give you enough energy if it is too acidic and needs the balance of alkaline foods.

God's balance is operating within your life whether you are aware of it or not. You cannot begin to create balance when steeped in negative energy. Like the pendulum that swings from one extreme to another, people often dip into the negative pole of life before they swing over to the extreme opposite pole until they make a reality check and choose to accept balance.

Extremes can bring confusion, chaos, and stagnation. The feelings of lethargy mixed with overwhelming sadness can freeze your mind and body.

On the other hand, the feelings of extreme positive energy can also throw you out of balance. Review your thoughts and actions for the past three days. Were you leaning toward the negative or were you too optimistic? Either can bring imbalance.

When you are feeling any of the negative emotions, do something for yourself that will be a treat. Allow it to be something that does not cause your body a reaction to an excess of sugar caused from eating comfort foods. Choose something that can lift you beyond your physical world and into your soul's wider perspective as in viewing it in the audience of your theatre while watching yourself upon your world stage.

We suggest using one of our guided visualizations that can take you out of your present mindset and help you ease over that bump in the road.

Whenever the mind wants to dwell on the past, or worry about the future, you are out of balance. **Worry thoughts are negative energy.** Do not allow them to pull you into a lower state of consciousness. Do not send worry thoughts to another as it will also pull them into a negative state as well.

Always make the choice to **take action** to bring your energy back into balance. Think of a happy song. Get up and dance. We suggest you go walk in nature or read an uplifting, inspirational book.

We continue to remind you that in viewing your life from your spirit's perspective—as if you are in the audience off Earth's stage—you will be able to see it without becoming emotionally involved within it. This is the best way for your spirit and soul to gain wisdom and to **release the control your emotions may have over you.**

There are some people whose soul has chosen for them to be born with an emotional imbalance called Bipolar where the wiring of the brain brings about great swings between manic joy and deep depression. Because it is a chemical imbalance, these people need the help of a professional who can advise a chemical solution to help keep the person in balance.

Remember also, if you have a Bipolar challenge, it is not a punishment nor a curse. Many good things will come to you because of this challenge, such as creating amazing things during the manic periods that would not have existed without your brain's wiring to bring to you special gifts to bless your planet.

Always... when you look for good, you shall find it. If you focus upon the challenge, it will grow harder. Lift up your mind and heart to God and give thanks for the wisdom your soul is gaining.

Guiding Principle # 3 — Trust

Trust is an awareness that your soul is essential in helping you create the life you desire.

When you try to "go it alone" or depend upon your own powers of creating without help from God and your soul, you are heading for failure and disappointment. Trusting in God and your soul requires a level of humility to know that no one is free from mistakes.

You need trust to become aware of the greater scheme of things which is what we are doing in this book. Whenever you feel locked within your problems, make a positive statement such as, "Beloved God. I place my trust in You to supply all my needs this day and every day of my life."

When you cannot see why something bad happens to good people, trust there truly is a divine purpose for it all. Trust will eventually open up your awareness of a bigger picture allowing for an "Ah ha!" moment when you discover the silver lining behind the dark cloud, when the "reasons" are revealed, when the question, "Why do things happen as they do?" becomes clear.

Trust allows you to look for the good in everything and everyone regardless of outward appearances. This does not mean to put blinders on. It means to have trust in divine guidance to show you how each person in your life serves a purpose in helping you grow closer to God.

Guiding Principle # 4 — Integrity

Integrity means using your mind and intuition with honor and respect for yourself and for others. It has the **intent** to do good and do no harm. Integrity requires you to be completely honest with yourself and with others.

When you practice integrity, you begin to realize how powerful you are as a creator of your own world. Your integrity will not allow you to create even the slightest deception within yourself or toward others.

You may also become more aware of a lack of integrity in others. Your intuition will warn you not to trust anyone who lacks integrity. This means to avoid people who demonstrate a lack of work ethics, of not giving 100% of their attention to the job, or of leaving early but charging for full time, of taking things that belong to the boss and say they have "earned it." Beware of these young souls, for they have not as yet experienced the consequences of their actions. Do not confide in them. Do not trust them in any way.

Although this warning seems to go against the principle of trust, it is clearly a matter of where and when to place your trust in others. Blind trust is for baby souls who will follow any leader unto death for a cause—good or bad. Blind trust will allow you to be swindled of your money—which in turn, may be part of the divine plan for your life to balance another life where perhaps you swindled another.

Guiding Principle # 5 — Self-Respect

Self-Respect refers to the acceptance of truth that you are a spark of the divine, a fragment of All-That-Is. This, of course, includes your soul manifesting through you within your physical world. Honoring your God-Spark means you do not allow another, including yourself to criticize, judge, mutilate or otherwise harm your body, mind or soul.

When you second-guess yourself or defer to another person's suggestions or ideas as better than your own, you have put your trust in another who does not know you as well as we do. Put your trust in the inspirations we send to you.

Many women tend to defer their choices to others whom they believe are smarter, or wiser, or have more knowledge than they do. Many give a piece of their soul away because they believe it is their mission to be of service to others.

They neglect their soul's purpose for their lives and instead, strive to create the visions and needs of others. This lack of self-respect is a denial of God's plan for their life. Each person's purpose is to become a co-creator with God.

We do not mean to throw out an examination of conscience where you admit to mistakes of wrong-doing or any lack of respect for others. It means instead to determine to do all things possible to honor your soul and spirit with honesty, integrity and self-respect.

Guiding Principle # 6 — Non-Judgment

The Rule of Non-Judgment discourages imposing one's opinions upon another.

This principle is hard for people who desire to serve others. Kind and sincere people can become the most judgmental, believing that it is their duty to point out the error of your ways, and perhaps to save you from your sins.

Gossip can be defined as having an opinion about another's personality, clothes, work ethics, mothering or fathering skills, etc. It may be your opinion but if it is also unkind and demeaning. It becomes an unjust judging of another and places yourself as better than the other, or of being the wiser and, therefore, beholding to point out the error of another's ways.

As you meditate daily, begin to let go of idle talk about others for too often you might have found yourself caught up in judging them or their situations. Even if it is done kindly as in making excuses for their behavior—it is still setting yourself up as a judge—and this is not good work.

More importantly–do not pass judgment on your own dear self.

We encourage you to put a guard on your mind and forbid the entry of any kind of negative thoughts. Give praise to self and speak words of encouragement and forgiveness.

Look at your reflection in the mirror and say, "I strive this day to become a pure reflection of God's truth, love, and joy."

Replace the concept of "judging" with discernment.

Discernment is the antidote for judgment. It allows you to look at a situation from all angles without acting on opinions or judgments. This quality of observation is valuable. We encourage you to pursue it before you decide as to the best direction for you to take.

Discernment allows you to help another in their decision-making process by offering alternative ideas—but only if they ask. Your observations may inspire them to examine their feelings and listen to their soul and spirit consciousness.

Discernment requires a detachment from the results of your decision-making process, knowing that your highest good will manifest no matter what choice you make.

To detach means to let go, to release and loosen the tendency to hold too close those we love out of fear of loss through abandonment or death. It means letting go of your wants and needs for another's well-being. It means avoiding your desire to jump up on their stage and redirect their soul's play by believing you have a better outcome for their story.

Some may believe if they practice detachment, it might mean they are less caring or even cold-hearted. It is just the opposite: Detachment means caring about someone so much that you respect their choices and do not interfere in their lives and even being reluctant to do so when asked.

Strive to become detached from any emotional outcome of another's choices. **This shows respect for their soul's need to learn from those choices.** It means you cannot volunteer your sage advice, nor even suggest your better way to handle a situation. Your judgment shows arrogance that you think you might know what is good, better or best for another.

Your soul's Council of Elders has known your stories since your birth from God. Who better to advise you?

We have seen those with heightened awareness of intuition, inner seeing and inner knowing when a person might predict a possible dangerous path. Every fiber of their being cries out to warn them. And yet, detachment prohibits it. All a sensitive person can do is bless the person by asking God to send them angels to lead them through their trials and bring them to a greater wisdom because of it.

Because every person has a story to tell on your planet's stage, it is not for you to change that story by intercepting what you can vividly see is a wrong path they have chosen to take.

Detachment means you need not worry about those you love. Remember that worry is a negative thought-form sent like an arrow to its target, and when its prickly, heavy energy hits, the person is struck down with it, reacting with a loss of energy shown in a slump of their shoulders. You do not want to do that to those you love. Worry thoughts are a perception that something bad is happening or is about to happen. Send a counter-worry thought of angels surrounding the person and light bulbs going off overhead as they hear our inspirations and lift themselves out of their difficulties. Then, their soul rejoices in the spurt of growth in consciousness. It is the gift of experience.

If a person is lacking financially, envision them dancing on the pot of gold at the end of a rainbow. In raising their consciousness out of fear or despair, you allow them to become aware of our inspirations to solve a seemingly unsolvable problem. This allows them to learn to trust the Divine Plan for their life. It means letting go of their perceived ideas for our better plan.

Now, of course, the Principle of Detachment does not apply in the same way to parents of underage children. Although it still applies to detaching emotionally when they disobey or get into trouble. Emotions can reflect the parent's need to control, or out of fear to save the child from harm, or to be seen as a responsible parent, or just to be right when being right has nothing to do with the child's needs and might reflect the parent's need for feeling power and control over another.

Again we say: parenting is always reflected in the soul's stage of development. This is why some old-soul children find themselves being the parent. It becomes the natural order of things.

Guiding Principle # 7 — Forgiveness

This principle is so often misunderstood. We hear, "I didn't do anything wrong. I have nothing to forgive." And, indeed, this is true as we have pointed out in the principle of **intent.**

Compassion dictates another side of forgiveness. Even if your intent was to do no harm, if another misinterpreted your words or actions for any unknown reason and you see that whatever you did or said brought pain and harm, you might choose compassion over seeking to clarify yourself.

This is not asking for forgiveness, but rather wisely becoming aware of your need to give comfort and love. Without words, an embrace can soothe a hurt and heal it instantly.

Anger that brings forth harsh words or even violence becomes too often the cause of misunderstandings and pain that require an apology and a need for forgiveness.

The abuse of alcohol or drugs can bring out the worst kind of emotional behavior. This can inflict harm upon others in which not only is an apology due but a determination to seek help in overcoming the cause of the behavior. Without that resolve, the apology is meaningless.

Marital abuse is an example of apologies that mean nothing when the act of violence is merely repeated again and again. Anger management came into existence because of the inability to express one's needs without resorting to violence.

All of this anger behavior reflects a very inexperienced soul who can only gain wisdom through sometimes painful behavior that apologies do not diminish and regret does not heal.

Guiding Principle # 8 — Now Time

You can only be in this moment as you experience the concepts you read in this book. More than likely, you have paused many times to contemplate an idea presented. You cannot experience anything except at this moment.

When you find yourself returning to something bad that happened in the past, you are experiencing that moment's emotional pain and discomfort all over again. This is the same with anxiety for any future "what if." Some say it is like paying rent on a house you never lived in! Each time you put yourself through the emotional trauma of the past or a supposed negative happening in the future, you are suffering without needing to do so.

We hear you ask how to stop watching the clock and stay in "now time." You cannot stop altogether, but you can decrease the amount of time spent in the vibrational energy of worry and anxiety. Through the raising of your conscious awareness, you will more quickly choose again whenever you find yourself worrying about the past or the future. The swings between positive and negative emotions are inherent within each human being who is trapped in the clutches of a planetary pull of time and space impacted with Pandora's run-away emotions.

Dear one: breathe deeply, go within and allow yourself to experience Now Time. It can be achieved by focusing fully on what you are doing in the moment without allowing your mind to wander to another task.

So many of you are used to multitasking, making it hard to keep focused on only one moment at a time without interference from your conscious-mind's prattle of so many other things. Only you can turn off the worry brought through the planet's negative polarity. **Command it to "Be Gone!"**

When Rae was teaching children from preschool to high school, she found that many children were suffering from Attention Deficit Disorder. Doctors put these children on prescribed medications which dulled their minds and closed off their ability to connect with their souls.

At that time, God had sent souls through a wave of indigo energy, so that they could be more in sync with the planet's raised energy. God sent advanced red, yellow, green, blue, indigo and violet souls who would help raise the consciousness of your human race.

Unfortunately, the indigo wave with its higher vibrating energy upset the usual educational program. These higher vibrating souls could not just sit, be quiet, and regurgitate what they were told. These souls entered with a mind and heart wide open to new ideas and the bigger picture. They began to question their teachers, challenge their parents, and strike out to follow their more advanced ideas that led them into politics or teaching careers or other occupations where suddenly you have many souls with indigo energy in your government in the body of women. They are not silent!

These souls are challenging the status quo by awakening many to seeing life differently. It is a challenge for them to continue to speak out against all the pressures for them to conform to the norm. Indigo energy never conforms to the norm. What a blessing this has been for your world.

Guiding Principle # 8 — Compassion

Compassion demonstrates the ability to express kindness, gentleness, and acceptance for another person's feelings, beliefs, and/or suffering. When someone is overly judgmental or critical of another, they demonstrate a lack of compassion. It does not necessarily mean they accept another's behavior when it is negative or destructive. Compassionate people realize how souls are doing the best they know in that given moment.

Compassion does not seek to know why the person feels or thinks or believes as he/she does. It does not seek to try to change the person, or to feel it their duty to teach them compassion.

Mother Theresa never asked the poor why they were poor. She did not make it her life's mission to teach them about prosperity and abundance. She did not scold them for being poor.

No. She demonstrated her unconditional love and compassion in accepting them as being perfect exactly as they were. She saw them with the compassion of God's love and ministered to their needs in her now moment.

And yet, we say unto you: her compassion was not automatically instilled within her emotional Pandora's box. Indeed, like all others, she had to practice using it by overcoming her own need for cleanliness and sweet-smelling bodies. She had to overcome her repulsion of the alcoholic's drunken urine-drenched odor.

Guiding Principle # 9 — Avoid Putting Your Expectations of Wisdom Upon Others.

Beloved souls—as you gain wisdom and knowledge through many lifetimes within a physical world, you must guard against expecting others to behave with the same wisdom that you have acquired. So often we find mature souls putting expectations on their co-workers to have the same work ethics they hold. Baby and young souls rarely exhibit this knowledge. And it is not for you to teach them.

In relationships, we also find expectations building into disharmony when a more experienced soul expects the partner to exhibit those characteristics of wisdom they have gained.

We say unto you, **expectations can be the death of a relationship.** Become aware of any you hold for another. Hold back your belief everyone "should" "could" be as you think, feel, or believe.

Guiding Principle # 10 — Oneness

Oneness recognizes that everything in both physical and non-physical dimensions is God's vibrating energy. It simply follows that we are all one within the majestic energy of God.

This is likely one of the most difficult concepts for humans to grasp because you live in a time/space dimension. You know separateness. You say, "You're you and I'm me." You may use the excuse that we, an archangel, cannot possibly understand what you as a human are experiencing.

Oneness negates that concept. We do understand, for we are within you with God. We feel as you feel. We breathe your breaths in and cleanse your body with each exhale.

The gift of separateness is to help you learn the art of creating. You cannot understand Oneness while in your human condition. You cannot perceive God as the Divine Source of all Energy and as One Mind that holds the thoughts of all minds. It is all right to accept this truth of feeling separate within the oneness.

Divine Love still fills your heart with joy.

Enlightenment can come to each of you when you meditate on these God-inspired Guiding Principles. Archangels are translators of the Mind of God. We are found in every ancient spiritual book. We have been at the right hand of God since the beginning of time. To grasp the realization that you are co-creators with the Master Creator is a giant step toward enlightenment.

Yet, with it comes great responsibility to use that divine energy only for good for yourself, for those in your world, for the good of your planet Earth, and for every materialized being within every planet within every galaxy within every universe surrounding your small planet.

Rejoice with us that we are one. All that we know, you know. All that you experience, we experience. When you cry, we cry. When you rejoice and give thanks, we sing along with you.

Let us sing and rejoice in our Oneness each day that we are given breath to do so. Even in the next dimension, we shall continue to give song in praising the One That Is All That Is.

Guiding Principle # 11 — Unconditional Love

Unconditional Love refers to a perfect God-love that has no strings attached, no "Shoulds" or "Oughts" or requirements that have to be met before this love is given.

Once you understand non-judgment, it becomes the natural order of things that leads to unconditional love for yourself and for all humankind.

Do not judge another by outward appearances. Remember, each soul comes with a different viewpoint garnered from lifetimes of experience—or from very little experience. A baby soul only seeks its own needs just as a baby would do. They fill their love relationships with conditions and expectations that someone will take care of all their needs.

Baby souls may express their needs by saying, "I'll love you... if you love me back... or if you are faithful... or if you will never hurt me." Another may say, "I'll do that favor for you if you do something for me." Or, "I expect you to show your love for me by bringing me gifts and flowers now and then." Or, "If you really loved me you would..."

It is disappointing to discover someone has strings attached to their love for you.

When you first come into your physical dimension, you look to your parents for unconditional love. Unfortunately, your parents are also looking for unconditional love from you. To some parents, that means instant obedience.

The withholding of love is a manipulative form of control. It is often used in relationships where anger can also be used as a control to force the partner to bend to another's needs.

Unconditional love must begin within self.

Now, obviously, you cannot use the concept of "loving yourself unconditionally" as meaning you have permission to self-indulge. The Rule of Balance is always in effect and it is said, "As you sow, so shall you reap." Loving yourself unconditionally means letting go of judging yourself and others.

With unconditional love, all other principles are added for the law of love encompasses all other laws.

We define abundance as having all your needs met. You define your needs, and then we supply the inspirations moment by moment as to how to meet those needs. It does not mean to have your needs met by others—but only by your own independent, ingenious self. When you understand this concept, you will be surprised at how all your needs are met easily, efficiently and with amazing speed.

The misperception of this truth comes when people look for abundance coming to them **from outside of themselves**, such as in winning the lottery or in suing someone.

Abundance is never associated with money. It is in the belief that God lovingly and carefully inspires you in how to solve a moment's puzzle. All you need to do is ask for how to have a need met and the know-how shall be given unto you.

It is the asking that confuses you. You think just asking will make it magically appear before you as though a gift from Heaven. You look for miracles that are really expecting some magic formula or special prayer or some magician's healing wand that will cure whatever troubles you.

And, sometimes, you do create just that. You find a special doctor or healer and miracles happen. Or your angel might whisper an idea in another's ear to answer your need. Even then, that person must decide if helping you is for their highest good. If not, they may choose not to follow God's inspiration.

Simply put, God does not supply your needs. You do. You are learning to be a co-creator with the Master Creator. If God supplied all your needs where would you learn to create?

Therein lies the misperception that it is God who supplies you with an abundance of material things. You are in a physical body within a physical dimension to gain the wisdom and knowledge in how to use God's energy to create physical matter. It is not God's job to supply solutions to questions or to create for you. That is your job as an apprentice under the Master Creator.

With your group of wise souls looking out for your specific needs through which you can gain knowledge and wisdom, they may present to you many challenges such as winning the lottery. It will only happen when your Council deems that the new opportunity would be of greatest benefit to you. The challenges presented often come as a surprise to the winners and often they question if it was all worth it.

Knowing the soul's previous lifetimes of choices and where they are on the maturity scale is also a factor in the help you receive from your Council.

The experience of sudden abundance can become a real challenge for a winner. The first lesson learned is that it has nothing to do with money **and everything to do with love and intent.**

All your needs are met each day when you trust God to inspire your soul on how to provide those needs. Abundance has nothing to do with how many dollars are in your pocket or in the bank.

People who found themselves short on cash tell stories of how after praying to God for help, they were suddenly gifted with extra dollars in the exact amount to take care of their need at that moment. They believe this proves God answers prayers.

It does not. It only proves that God will inspire you as to how to produce the abundance you seek. It reminds you of that money you had stashed in your pocket and then forgot about it.

God always answers prayers—just not always in the way you might want or expect. In this case, God was trying to show your soul the truth about abundance.

People will insist that God rescued them. Many stories arise of those who did not get their prayers answered and had to take drastic measures like bankruptcy to solve their lack of income, or indeed, by robbing a bank! When they ended up in jail, they cried out, "Why didn't you save me God?"

An inexperienced soul may act through greed, manipulation, and the seeking of power and control over others. The Principle of Balance has a way of turning things upside-down and inside-out. People who seek power and money without using integrity or love can eventually find themselves powerless and at the mercy of others.

There are those who may use the excuse that they are re-living bad Karma, or that God is punishing them for some misdeed in some long-ago lifetime. It is not so!

Karma is simply the natural law of balance. Anything out of sync within the universe will seek to balance itself. Your soul needs to experience all extremes of those pendulum swings until finally in its old age, the soul becomes centered and finds true inner peace and joy.

We have said repeatedly that the emotions flowing from the state of love are poured forth from the Creator God. Love encompasses all within and without in a broad embrace of everyone and everything. God is pure in Its intention and purpose. It is joy embodied in a bright light that uplifts and steadies and fills you with hope and courage.

True unconditional love becomes your continuing search within your planet. You look for God in others and cannot find It. You look for It in earthly pleasures and cannot find It. You look for It in the mirror and cannot find It.

You look in all the wrong places. Look within. God is hiding right there ready to pour forth the balm of unconditional love all over you. God is waiting for you to open your arms to embrace the purest love you shall ever know.

God is waiting. God is patient. God's love will never go away.

Summary of the Guiding Principles

Each guiding principle merges as one into the Law of Love. With Prudence, you also see Balance and Integrity activated simultaneously. When you activate these Principles, it is like laying patio blocks that lead to your inner sanctuary's garden of beauty and peace. You water the flowers of prosperity and manifest amazing things even beyond your imagination.

You have a saying that, "Necessity is the mother of invention." It is true. Rather than try to begin with the thought of "wanting" something, begin instead with the thought of "What do I need to do to solve this problem?"

For example, if you are having trouble paying the bills, rather than focus on winning the lottery, visualize obtaining the perfect job or jobs that can increase your income and allow you to pay your bills easily and on time. Keep your mind open to new ideas. Be willing to step out of your safe box in letting go of the fear of lack to experience something new and exciting.

All things created remain within the mind of God. Since you are in that Mind, you have all things, too. Understand there is far more beneath the surface than you perceive.

As you go back and study these principles, we suggest you make a list of any you might wish to explore through your daily experiences. We suggest you concentrate on studying one principle for the next seven days. Observe the people around you as to their practice of this principle. Write your observations in your scientific journal. You may find you can easily pick out the younger souls from the older ones. This alone can be comforting as well as enlightening.

We remind you: You are God's Lamplighter. Each time you contemplate any of these principles, you raise not only your consciousness, but that of many others for your thoughts radiate out like beacons of light.

Rejoice and be glad. Your planet shall be saved. You are creating peace in this moment with each beat of your heart as you breathe in your love of God and breathe out gratefulness and joy.

Angels attend to you. Know this is so. Call upon us each day. We can only serve when asked. Ask and it shall be given unto you.

Chapter 23
A New Earth

You, dear reader, now have the tools to change your personal world for the better, and in so doing you will raise your consciousness, which will also raise that of others, which will lead to the inspiration on how to heal your planet. When you lift your mind and heart out of cynicism, anxiety, fear and doubt, you can begin to use your creative mind in sync with the divine mind to help bring about a wonderful, enlightened world, free of pollution and free of destructive human tendencies.

During the destructive pandemic you discovered that pollution allowed people to see mountains that had been obliterated by smog. Lakes and rivers that could no longer sustain life were suddenly filled with fish. What greater way to shout out "Global Warming!"

We have shown you how to imagine what you desire, how to hold fast to the vision, how to remain steady and faithful until you see it manifested into some form of reality in your physical world.

God has no limit on time as you do. Whatever you visualize daily within your inner sanctuary can seem to be a subliminal vision but not a reality. And yet, when it is "time," it may rise to the surface and become a desire that you can bring into physical reality.

Rae's inner sanctuary with white carpeting in a glass house with bookshelves on either side of a fireplace became a reality when she and her husband remodeled his modest ranch home. She had not realized she had created it exactly as she had envisioned it twenty years earlier until the renovations were done.

Trust is a key element in the process of being a co-creator with God. Trust that all things are possible and it shall be as you command.

We encourage you to continue practicing the kind of imagery offered here. We encourage you to take time to listen within, to go to your Inner Sanctuary to create your personal world of peace, harmony and love.

Imagine your planet at peace, in harmony with nature, and loved by its inhabitants enough to heal it. We urge you to picture a world free of pollution for the children of generations to come.

You are powerful co-creators with all the energy of God at your fingertips. You can move mountains. You can save your planet. You can use these tools to do it without spending a dime or going anywhere except within where the power of God is waiting for you to release all doubts and fears, to open your willingness to become as little children and use your joyful imagination!

You, dear reader, are also a translator of God ideas. You are given unique and wonderful inspirations to be made manifest in your world. Do not allow negative emotions to block the wonderful works you are inspired by God to create. Ideas are sent directly to your mind to bring forth like a newborn child into your beautiful world. Your entire life as a soul is to do just that. Know that with each new and exciting idea that stirs your emotions, it enlightens your mind and pushes you to explore the mind of God within you asking you to become the channel through which an idea is born.

We cannot say it more clearly—you are created by God to be a partner, a co-creator, a channel through which all things good and beautiful are inspired for you to turn it into a reality to see, touch and feel, and then to step back and bask in the joy of creating.

Through this book, may your light shine brightly. May your soul quicken and awaken to the calling to greatness.

We ask you to become the 100th Monkey by lifting your world out of darkness and into divine light.

We ask you to become God's Lamplighter. Begin today to spread humor and laughter, smiles and encouragement to others, to give praise and appreciation for all you meet as you find more and more reasons each day to rejoice and give thanks to God.

With great love for all humanity, we are...
Raphael

Acknowledgements

I wish to thank God for the privilege of channeling an archangel. It has brought me so many blessings. It has been a joy to transcribe the thoughts of this great being of divine light. I have learned so much and hope you have as well.

I also wish to thank all my friends for their wonderful support and encouragement in writing this book. It has not been an easy journey, but we were persistent and found our way to the end of the task.

We encourage you to gather friends to discuss Raphael's wisdom within this book. Perhaps one person in the group could read aloud the guided meditations so that the others could concentrate on the visualization.

From living with this wonderful teacher for so many years, I'm amazed and eternally grateful for all the gifts of friendship, creativity and beauty that constantly fill my life.

About the Author

Betty Rae retired from teaching eight years earlier because her husband wanted her to join him in his retirement. At first she resisted, saying she loved teaching her eighth-grade Language Arts students.

While renovating their home in Michigan, she fell off a ladder and broke her back, keeping her from teaching for a couple months. When she returned, the students were undisciplined from having so many substitutes. It took Betty Rae a couple of weeks to restore order. At the end of the school year, she retired.

It was then her spiritual gifts blossomed and she began channeling Archangel Raphael, writing metaphysical books, teaching classes and opening her home to welcome seekers in twice monthly open houses where she channeled Raphael.

After the passing of her husband, Betty Rae moved to Florida where she now resides. In her eighties, she continues to channel the archangel, but no longer charges for the messages. She says it is time to give back all the blessings she has been given.

Below is Betty Rae's web page so that if you are reading this book after she has passed from this world, you will know why you cannot reach her! But if you do contact Betty Rae, Raphael will be made avaialble to speak with you.

Her web page is
www.angelbettyraeandraphael.com
Her YouTube Channel is
www.youtubeaskraphal/bettyrae
Her Radio Show is www.w4wnradio.com/askraphael
It airs each Tuesday at noon and is also found on iHeart Radio

Other Books by Betty Rae

Letters from a Guardian Angel. (Available only on Betty Rae's web page).

Life in 3Dimensions: Physical, Spiritual, and Physical. (Available only on Betty Rae's web page).

Bigotry—Book 1—The Anita Lyn Series—a novel. (Available through Amazon).

Greed—Book 2—The Anita Lynn Series—a novel. (Available through Amazon).